D1256063

Chromatic Harmony

CHROMATIC HARMONY

Justine Shir-Cliff

Stephen Jay

Donald J. Rauscher

Fp THE FREE PRESS, NEW YORK

A DIVISION OF THE MACMILLAN COMPANY

Printed in the United States of America

Library of Congress Catalog Card Number: 64-23079

Second printing May 1966

The authors dedicate this work to

Margo, Danny, Naomi, Ronnie and *Matthew Jay*

and

Mary and *Frances Rauscher*

Preface

THIS BOOK is written for serious students of music. We hope that those whose obligation it is to learn, to perform, or to teach will find it useful. It is the result of the learning, performing, and teaching experience of the authors as influenced by the learners, performers, and teachers with whom we have been and are associated.

Literate musicianship requires an intimate familiarity with the harmonic concepts which brought music to the threshold of contemporary practice and it is our aim to present the subject in as practical and unopinionated a manner as possible.

Three authors undertook this work because as members of the faculty at the Manhattan School of Music we are happily accustomed to cooperative effort. Only a lack of precedent and the inevitable unwieldiness which would result prevented the active participation of many others. We who happen to be named as authors gratefully acknowledge the valuable advice, encouragement, and unfailing good spirits of our colleagues.

J. S., S. J., D. J. R.

New York City, 1964

Contents

To the Teacher

THIS TEXT naturally presupposes a background in traditional diatonic practice. The behavior of tones and chords within an unchanging tonality, modulation to related keys, and the function and nomenclature of non-harmonic tones must be familiar to those who would understand chromatic harmony. Also beneficial will be an acquaintance with the elements of form, basic counterpoint as reflected in harmonic voice-leading, and the differences and similarities of texture, notation, and arrangement in the conformation of music for the various media of performance.

Terminology, ever a bugbear to musicians attempting to reduce to verbiage the far more subtle language of music, must be agreed upon. The authors have devised no new terms, invented no new formulae, and conceived no arbitrary design of the musical universe into which must be fitted the diverse and mysterious vagaries of art.

Figured bass symbols are used as they were understood by our musical predecessors to whom they were more effective prompters of performance than our more specific contemporary notation. Roman numerals occur where they identify significant diatonic relationships. Where the tonality is so thoroughly obscured that their use would be superfluous the letter names of chord roots are given and the establishment of a purely theoretical relationship to a key center is not attempted.

Non-harmonic tones are a continual problem because it is difficult to be consistent about a line of division between two concepts: that all tones other than root, third, fifth, and seventh are non-harmonic; or that sixths, ninths, elevenths and thirteenths are admissible to the inner circle of acceptable chord tones. Our guide is common practice. Passing tones, neighbor notes, suspensions, anticipations, escape tones (*échappées*), changing tones (*cambiata*) are readily definable. A definition of the appoggiatura, (a rather ambiguous term in Italian derived from *appoggiare*: to support; to lean; to prop) must be established. In this text, non-harmonic tones which are approached by leap and resolved by step to more stable tones are termed appoggiatura. Contrary to various arbitrary definitions, the accented or unaccented metrical position and the relative direction of the leap or stepwise resolution of the tones are not significant factors in their identification.

The text proper attempts to describe and illustrate chromatic usage and the workbook provides opportunities for practical application, testing, and experimentation. The division into chapters isolating individual aspects of chromaticism permits the teacher to interject review or examination sessions at any point and to adapt the study to any college calendar.

The descriptive and explanatory material of the text is presented as concisely as possible, but each chapter of the workbook contains more subjects for drill, review, analysis and practical and creative application of the devices under discussion than may reasonably be required of every group of students. It will be found that it is possible to assemble two or more comprehensive assignments for each chapter.

Just as a knowledge of diatonic harmony is a prerequisite to the study of chromatic harmony, so it is essential that each chapter of this book be thoroughly assimilated before a subsequent chapter is undertaken. It is especially important that the chromatic dominant seventh chord be mastered, for this semidiatonic structure is the most frequently encountered chromaticism and the one to which most of the more complicated occurances are directly related.

Musical passages from various media of performance were chosen to demonstrate the points of discussion, but each teacher is advised to utilize additional excerpts from the literature which is most familiar to the students whose guidance is his responsibility.

As every teacher knows, no text answers all questions. This text is intended to be an aid, to offer definitions of procedures, and to do so without prejudice, arbitrariness, or condescension. The joy of writing this book lies in the expectation that it will help good teachers to teach better.

Chromatic Harmony

I

Chromaticism

THE TERM "CHROMATIC" is understood by musicians to refer to music which includes tones which are not members of the prevailing scale, and also as a word descriptive of those individually non-diatonic tones.

These are the definitions which are subscribed to in the chapters which follow. It is not intended, however, that the student be led to believe that all music is either diatonic or chromatic. Musical expression has been a basic human impulse since the dawn of time, in all eras and areas. It has taken shape in many different scale patterns and gradations of pitch, all of which cannot be notated in our Western method of notation. Even the familiar and important differences in pitch between equal and just temperament cannot be represented in the clefs, the lines and spaces, and the sharps, flats, and naturals to which we are restricted. The history of our notation is long and usually goes unquestioned but its deficiencies are many. In spite of the undeniable fact that it has served to preserve the works of the composers who reached the highest levels of communication it should not be permitted to limit modern inventiveness or the understanding of non-Western, primitive, or ancient musical expressions.

Our present concern is with the harmonic and melodic vocabulary of eighteenth and nineteenth-century Western music. This is the organization of tones and tonal relationships which won for music the stature it enjoys today, for the concert hall did not exist before this union of melody and harmony was established. Is it unreal to assume that the attention given to music, separate from the salon, the church, the theater, and the ceremony, was the enticing and attention-holding harmonic variety then in ascendancy?

There are many dedicated, skilled, and imaginative musicians of our day who, unable to accept any rejection of this technic, direct their efforts toward an unpredictable further development of tonal music. Other musicians whose concern is with the commercial aspects of the profession, making a direct appeal to the undescriminating elements of the general public, seldom employ more than elementary devices of chromatic harmony. Many serious composers who write radical contemporary music do so in revolt against and in direct and discouraged reaction to the logical and unfailingly communicative music of the best nineteenth-century composers. Note that modern concert programs rarely fail to include nineteenth-century music. The continuing popularity of this music is of course due to many factors, not the least among them is the dramatic and personal appeal of romanticism, the advent of virtuosity in performance and composition, and the simultaneous activity of an astonishing number of supremely creative musicians. Virtuosity is now almost commonplace and modern creative musicians view the romantic scene with apprehension, for it is not their own. But creativity is still with us, as vital as ever, seeking a comparable base of operation.

The study of nineteenth-century music should be undertaken for the acquisition of the skills required for understanding its language—essential for all who would perform—and for its historical importance as the language of a period in the history of music which reached a very high peak and which continues as a strong influence on contemporary practice.

The adoption of the major and minor modes in the seventeenth century made possible the ultimate development of chromaticism. Subtle colorations of melody and chord resolutions and the intermingling of keys are effective only when they are obvious departures from, or expansions of, a consistent and clearly discernible tonal center of gravity. The major mode is most readily accepted by the ear, its source in the harmonic series of overtones being a natural phenomenon, and this major and the three theoretical forms of the minor scale are now commonplace outgrowths of Renaissance practice.

In diatonic music all tones are members of the prevailing major or minor mode. (This refers to the period under study, not to others in which the Greek origin of the word 'diatonic' may be invoked to justify its use in other connections.) Chromaticism is a departure from the diatonic. The study of harmony has long been divided into the separate survey of the diatonic and chromatic processes, a concept which has no historical validity. It is justifiable only because of the urgent necessity for a thorough appreciation of the behavior of tones within the tonal center of influence. The principles of voice leading (inseparable from counterpoint), the definition and function of non-harmonic tones, and the inherent tendencies of individual tones and chords to resolve must be mastered before the complexity of their translation into chromaticism can be understood. The diatonic and chromatic processes are rarely separated in music, for there has never been a period of diatonic composition followed by a period of chromatic composition, but it is not rare to find passages in which they are separated *within* a musical texture.

The persistently popular waltz king, Johann Strauss, shows how chromatic tones can be superimposed over a most elementary diatonic harmonic accompaniment, the tonic and dominant seventh chords.

EXAMPLE 1. J. Strauss: *Voices of Spring*

Frederick Chopin, unsurpassed master of romantic piano music and master harmonist, has left us enough illustrations of chromaticism to fill more than one textbook. From many quotable examples one is selected to demonstrate the use of chromatics as accompaniment to a diatonic melody.

Example 2. Chopin: *Prelude,* Op. 28 No. 21

Passages which use chromatic tones in both melody and harmony are more prevalent in the literature than those which illustrate the theoretical concept of diatonic vs. chromatic. The melodic origin of chromatic tones in the elaboration and intensification of the contours of lines of melody is seen in the next work quoted. It is part (measure 18-20) of a prelude by J. S. Bach, to whom every principle of musical expression was apparently as natural as breathing. In this instance he has chosen to present four simultaneous individually distinguished voices. The upper voice, soprano, is given a melody which is characterized by descending half-steps. The bass moves more deliberately and features dissonant and unexpected leaps, strongly contrasting with the chromatic scale of the soprano. The tenor voice sounds a sequential melody and the alto, since three melodic devices have been usurped by the other three parts, contributes a melody whose personality is dependent upon the absence of conspicuous stepwise motion, leaps, or sequences. It is further distinguished by its unresolved extension to the cadence in F.

EXAMPLE 3. J. S. Bach: *Well Tempered Clavier,* Prelude I, Book II

Each of the fragments quoted above is a quotation out of context. The compositions from which they were extracted should be studied in their entirety, for each has won a place in the catalogue of long-term listenable music.

It should also be noticed that each of these three composers has chanced to use the twelve tones of the chromatic scale in the short sections shown.

Three clearly differentiated styles are illustrated in these excerpts, demonstrating that the chromatic vocabulary is an important element in the still attractive dance music of a bygone era (and, though not illustrated, also our own), the rich and adventurous world of Romanticism, and the eternal universe of Johann Sebastian Bach.

It is not possible to live through a day of exposure to practice, concert, radio, theater, television, or movie music (or even to our singing, whistling, humming selves or neighbors) without being reminded of our obligation as musicians to be versed in musical technic.

II

The Chromatic Dominant Seventh Chord

MANY CHROMATIC CHORDS are simply diatonic harmonies of another key. The dominant seventh chord is found in an uncountable number of situations in which it is not the dominant of the prevailing key, but where its undeniable tendency toward resolution is utilized to emphasize the non-tonic chords of the second, third, fourth, fifth, and sixth degrees of major scales. Most of these secondary triads are frequently preceded by the diatonic seventh chord whose root lies a perfect fifth above or a perfect fourth below (VI^7 to II, II^7 to V, III^7 to VI), and chromatic dominants are the result of alteration of the quality of the secondary seventh chords. The II^7 to V, for example, becomes a chromatic progression when the chord third of the II^7 is raised a half step, for its sound is then indistinguishable, except for the previously established tonality, from the sound of V^7 to I in the dominant key.

EXAMPLE 4

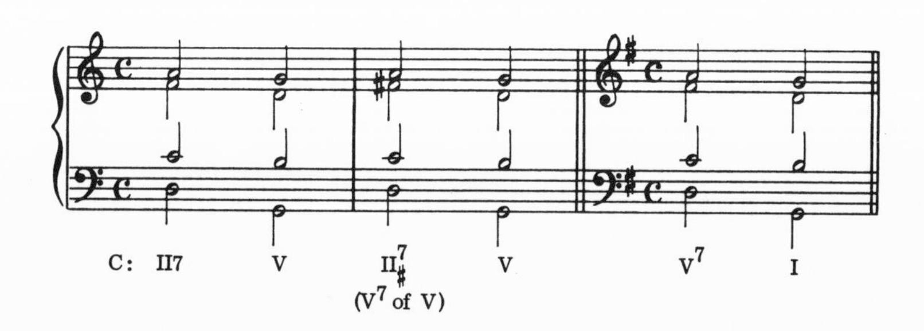

Other chromatic dominants have similar diatonic sources:

EXAMPLE 5

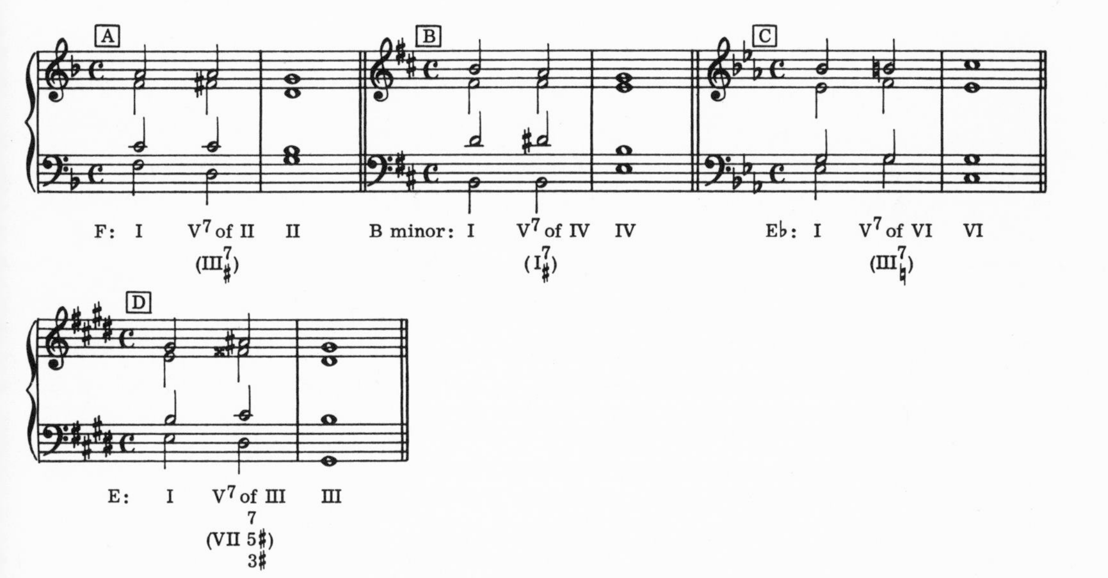

The resolution of V^7 of V may be delayed in established or new keys by the interjection of the tonic $\frac{6}{4}$ chord between the chromatic dominant and its destination. It should be noted that the tendency toward resolution is not contradicted—only postponed.

EXAMPLE 6

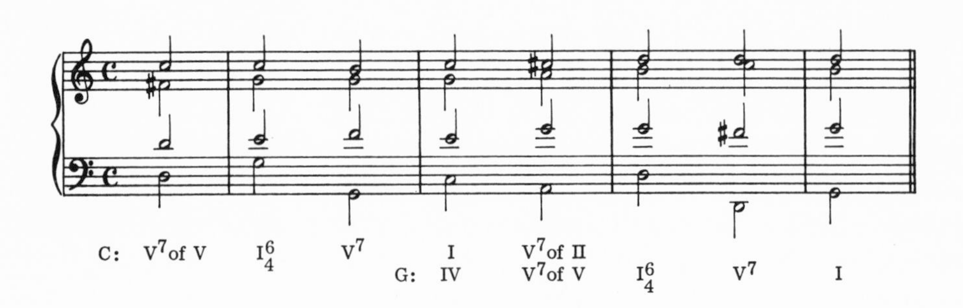

The triad on the seventh degree of the scale, diminished in quality and therefore not a tonal center, obviously cannot receive the attentions of a dominant. In the minor mode only V^7 of III (major), IV, V, and VI are available since II, diminished in quality as is VII in both major and minor, is the center of no tonality. (The harmonic minor scale is here considered the basis for diatonic harmony in the minor mode.)

All the attributes and procedures of the diatonic dominant seventh chord accompany its transference to other than its own tonality and it may be well to review its characteristics here.

EXAMPLE 7

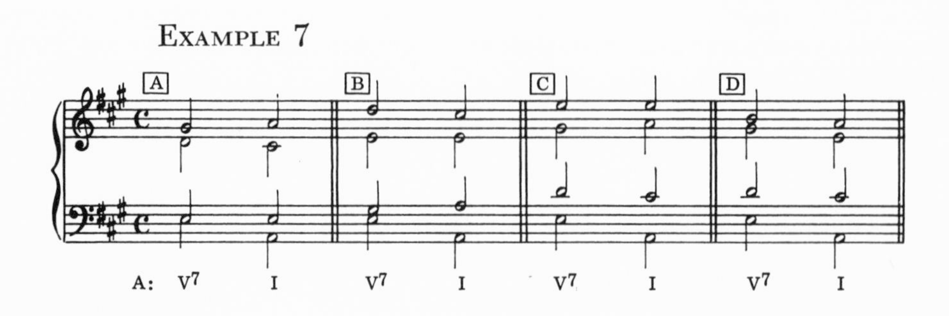

Example 7 shows the four possible arrangements of the dominant seventh chord in root position in A major.* When the third (a), seventh (b) or root (c) is the upper tone it is wise to omit the chord fifth and double the root, forming an *incomplete* dominant seventh chord. A complete (root, third, and fifth) tonic chord is thus best approached. Experimentation will show that if these dominants are complete with all four tones a complete tonic chord cannot be attained without contradiction of the natural tendency toward resolution of the tones and intervals of the dominant seventh. First and foremost among these tendencies is the resolution of the tritone (augmented fourth and diminished fifth). In Example 7 (a, b, and c), the tritone is perfectly resolved: augmented fourths outward by step, diminished fifths inward by step. In Example 7 (d), the leading tone of the key, whose impulse to resolve upward a half step is almost undeniable, is resolved down a third. This is admissible only when it is neither uppermost or lowermost voice, usually when the fifth of the dominant chord is in soprano. Another way of pointing out this principle is to say that the leading tone resolves up and the chord seventh resolves down, each by step. In Example 7 (a, b, c, and d), the tones which are not part of the tritone, the doubled roots, resolve as unobtrusively as possible: one does not move at all but remains as a stationary common tone, and the other, the bass tone, moves from root to root. In Example 7 (d), and in all similar arrangements in which it is present, the fifth of the dominant resolves by step to the root of the tonic.

These procedures are effective when the dominant seventh is either diatonic or chromatic, and four voice versions such as those illustrated should be borne in mind whenever analysis, composition, or arranging is attempted. Although most composers do not limit themselves to the strict choral style it is the one style in which the harmony of all simpler or more complex tonal music can be clearly realized. It is the most practical

* *The upper and lower voices are the important factors. The alto and tenor voices may be in close or open position.*

point of departure for the understanding of the technics of diatonic and chromatic harmony.

Example 8 shows a simple application of these principles:

EXAMPLE 8

Example 8 (a) is a picture of the harmonic structure of Example 9 (a). Example 8 (b) shows the chord connections underlying Example 9 (b). It should be noted that melodic lines or elaborations need not be shown: a clear harmonic picture is all that is required.

EXAMPLE 9a. Schubert: *Litany for the Feast of All Souls*

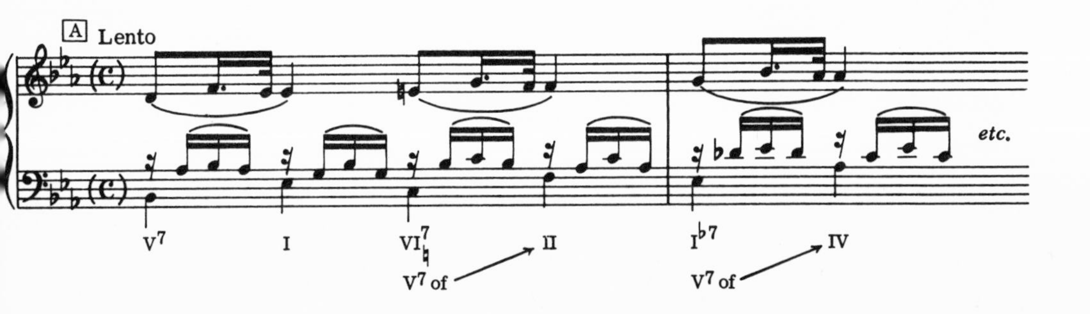

EXAMPLE 9b. von Weber: *Invitation to the Dance*

The chromatic dominant seventh chord illustrates the most crucial aspects of the management of other chromatic chords: the leading-tone function of chromatically raised tones (as in V^7 of II, III, V, VI),

EXAMPLE 10

and the tendency of chromatically lowered tones to descend (as in V^7 of IV):

EXAMPLE 11

Each major and minor triad of the diatonic scale may be preceded by the chromatic dominant triad or seventh chord with which it can share the dominant-tonic relationship. If the student will prove this statement by writing the resolutions of chromatic dominant sevenths to II, III, IV, V, and VI in a variety of keys it will be seen that even when the tonal center is not disturbed the twelve tones of the chromatic scale are with us.

III

Inversions of the Chromatic Dominant Seventh Chord

INVERTED chromatic dominant seventh chords are frequently found in the music of the nineteenth century because the need for melodic fluency was strongly felt even in that very harmonic (as opposed to the polyphonic) era. Stepwise melodic motion is more common than non-stepwise motion, and inversions make stepwise bass lines possible when roots, as is their wont, move by leap.

Example 12 is a fragment of a famous operatic aria which features chromatic dominants in their first inversion. This Example shows diatonic triads preceded by their own dominants, and their $^6_5$ positions bring about the ascending chromatic scale steps in the first four quoted measures of bass.

EXAMPLE 12. Verdi: *Rigoletto*, "La donna e mobile"

The melody is thus able to leap from the roots of the chromatic dominants to the roots of the chords to which they resolve; the more ordinarily seen bass movement from root to root is transferred to the upper voice without producing the crassness of parallel octaves. The "hidden octaves" (the F sharps in measure two and the G sharps in measure four, approached in similar motion and by leap in the upper voice are hidden octaves) are forbidden in strictly contrapuntal constructions but are common in the works of nineteenth-century composers and can also be found in the productions of their predecessors when the texture is essentially harmonic.

Robert Schumann, in Example 13 shows a more radical departure from contrapuntal practice and another use of the chromatic dominant seventh in first inversion.

EXAMPLE 13. Schumann: *Grillen*, Op. 12 No. 1

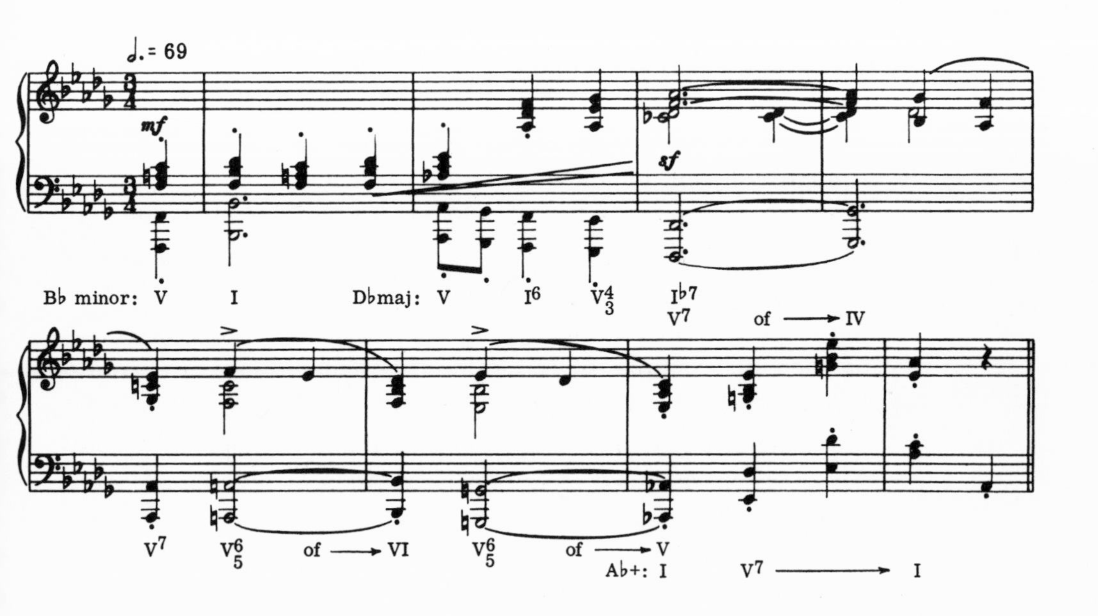

Example 13 modulates. It begins in B flat minor but by measure two has been deflected toward the relative major. The A flat on the first beat of measure two contradicts the leading tone of the minor mode and as inevitably as though guided by the law of gravity proclaims the relative major key. The chromatic dominant of the subdominant in measure three intensifies the effect and establishes the cadence in the dominant of the relative major (measure seven) as a logical point of repose. The inverted chromatic dominants in measures five and six intensify this effect. They are unstable and obviously dependent upon their resolution for justification. The tonal centers emphasized in this short passage are pointed up by chromatic dominants in root position and first inversion. The use of $\frac{6}{5}$ chords points out the intermediate degree of dominance they possess. The first (measure five) is readily accepted as a decorative embellishment. The second (measure six), because of the imminence of the cadence, functions as a true dominant. Strict counterpoint does not allow the occurrence of the opposite motion parallel octaves (E flat to A flat in both outer voices) found at the cadence of Example 13, but it will be seen that the highest E flat is superfluous to the harmonic structure. The four tone chord is complete and correctly resolved without it and its presence is due to the composer's desire to dramatize the cadence. Compare with the similar but not identical cadence of Example 9 b, page 28.

The second inversion of the chromatic dominant seventh chord, though less frequently used than the $^6_5$ position, is also a useful means of attaining stepwise bass lines. The fifth in bass may resolve down or up by step, but the downward resolution as seen in Example 14 is far more common than the upward turn. Ludwig van Beethoven's first published string quartet provides the example and illustrates the chromatic V^4_3 of II and III. The lines are assigned to the instruments in the customary way: Violin I is soprano, Violin II is alto, Viola is tenor and Violoncello is bass. The dominant $^4_3$ of II appears on the third beat of measure two and in sequence the dominant $^4_3$ of III on the third beat of measure four. In both instances the first of the pair of eighth notes is an accented passing tone and the second eighth note is the bass of the harmony. In measure four the tones of the ascending melodic minor scale are involved and the normal minor third of the VI chord is raised to its major form. The region of A minor is emphasized by means of the III, V of III, III progression in measures five and six but the expected cadence in the dominant (of F major) key is strongly asserted in the measures which follow.

EXAMPLE 14. Beethoven: Quartet, Op. 18 No. 1, Scherzo

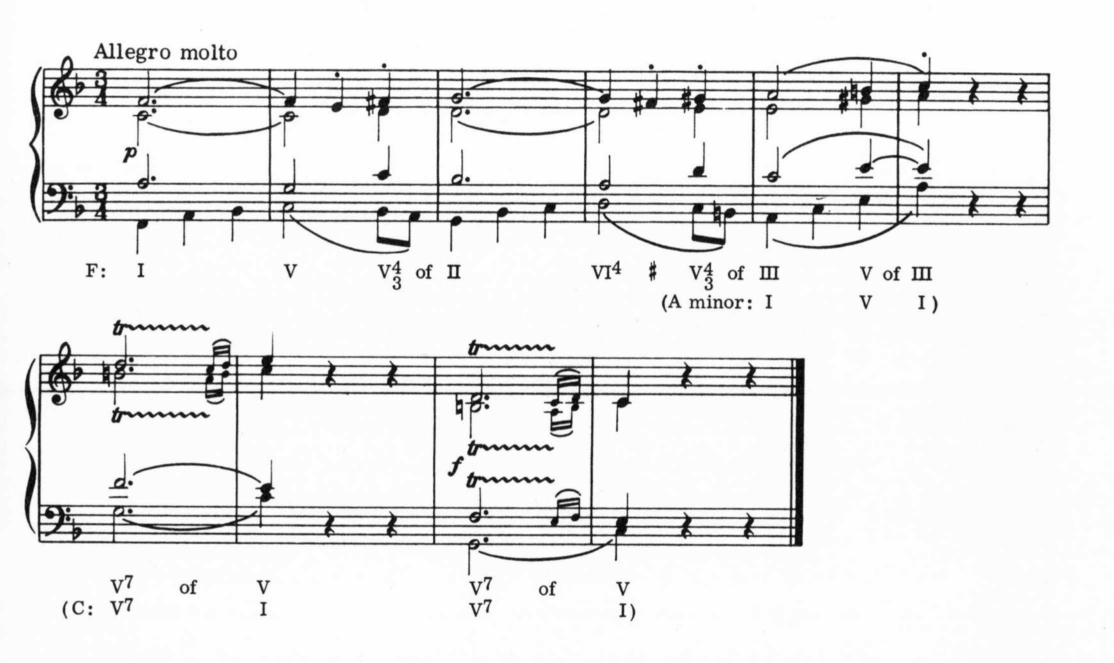

The upward resolution of the bass tone of the chromatic dominant $^4_3$ need not be illustrated because its movement is identical to diatonic usage: when the bass tone in the chord of resolution is the tone to which the seventh would normally resolve the seventh may resolve up by step or by leap to another chord tone usually down a fourth.

The one form of the dominant seventh chord, diatonic or chromatic, which never produces a cadential effect is the third inversion. It invariably resolves to the first inversion of the chord of resolution or to another non-tonic functioning chord. Another fragment from the string quartet repertoire illustrates the similarity of function and of voice leading in the resolution of inverted chromatic dominants. In Example 15, the last eighth-note chord of measure one is the dominant $^4_2$ of IV, the second eighth-note chord of measure two is the dominant $^4_3$ of IV, and the fourth eighth-note chord of measure two is the dominant $^6_5$ of IV.

EXAMPLE 15. Haydn: Quartet, Op. 76 No. 2, First movement

In the resolution of each of these chromaticisms the individual tones of the chord obey inevitable natural laws in common with diatonic dominants. The leading tones (F sharp) in Violin I and Violoncello resolve upward by step. The chord sevenths (C) in Violoncello and Viola resolve downward by step. The roots and fifths, less volatile and demanding than the dissonant elements of the chord, resolve less predictably but by step or are repeated as common tones.

Chromatic harmony, like diatonic harmony, cannot be understood or mastered unless the tendency and function of each individual tone is comprehended within the domain of each individual tonality. Chromatic dominants, inverted or not, afford clear examples of the management of tones not included in the scale indicated by the key signatures. More subtle, remote, and complicated chromatic constructions will be incomprehensible until the behavior of chromatic dominants in tonal environments is as familiar as A B C.

IV

Consecutive Chromatic Dominants

SERIES OF CHORDS whose roots move through the cycle of fifths are staples of diatonic structure, and their translation into chromatic terminology is hardly less obvious or useful.

The one exceptional procedure in the resolution of tones from chromatic dominant to chromatic dominant is the contradiction of the upward tendency of the leading tone. When resolved to a dominant quality chord whose root is the expected tonic, the leading tone—the third of the chromatic dominant—surrenders its natural obligation and resolves down a half step to become a downward resolving seventh. This principle is clearly shown in Example 16. The short quotation given here is a reduction of a transitional episode which ushers in only one of the work's many technically, musically and spiritually convincing scenes.

EXAMPLE 16. Brahms: Symphony No. 4, Finale

This essentially three voice structure emerges from the orchestral score to which five woodwind instruments and five sections of stringed instruments contribute their tones. The dominant triad of the prevailing tonality is followed by the tonic bass tone, but the tonic triad is replaced by the dominant quality chord of V7 of A. V7 of A resolves, not to A, but to A,V7 of D. V7 of D resolves to V7 of G, and V7 of G to V7 of C. The chord which follows, V7 of F, is spelled enharmonically: A sharp instead of B flat. The reason for the augmented sixth notation of the minor seventh of the chord will be obvious to those who have studied the chromatic scale. The fifth scale step, the dominant tone of the prevailing tonality is customarily not chromatically altered in the downward direction: composers have unanimously preferred to preserve its appearance as the leading tone of the dominant key. It is also worthy of notice that the sequential *sharp* to *natural* progression of melodic tones would be broken and the atmosphere of E minor disrupted if B flat instead of A sharp were used.

The composer, has, undoubtedly according to plan, *established,* or more exactly in this instance *reestablished,* the tonal center at the point in the cycle of fifths at which the diminished fifth or augmented fourth leap in the bass occurred. It will be seen, if extensive analysis of music literature is undertaken, that this is common practice: the change of quality in the interval of the bass motion supports a change of quality and consequent tonal orientation in the harmony.

The management of four voices in consecutive dominants is demonstrated in the next quotation, and it also offers a rather typical illustration of how composers have used harmonic commonplaces as accompaniment to melodic creativity.

EXAMPLE 17. Tchaikovsky: *Romeo and Juliet*

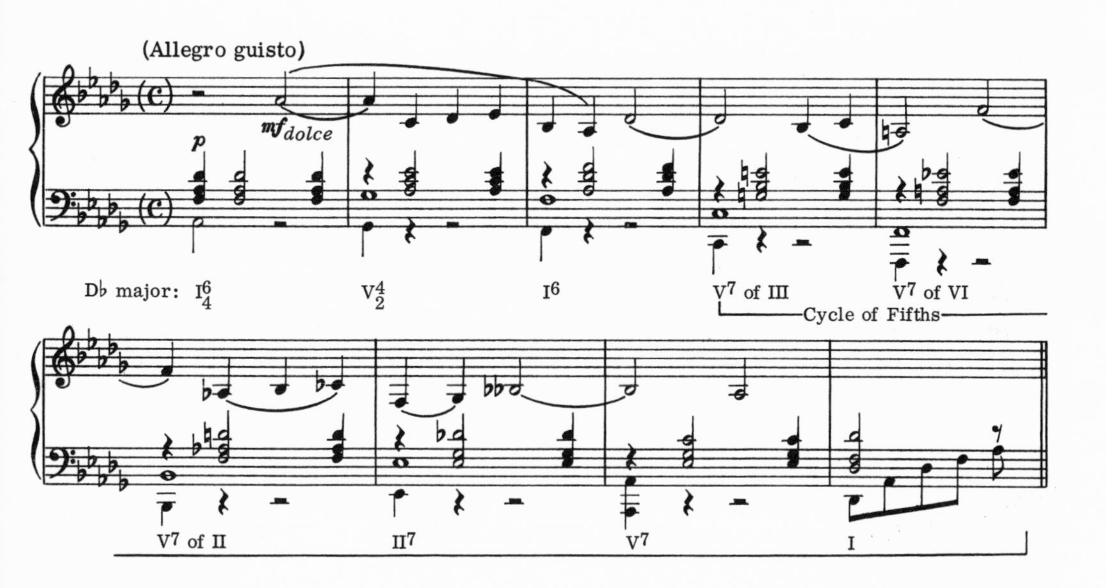

This passage appears to be a five-voice structure. An ornate melody is superimposed over four supporting voices. The melody is chromatic, stylistically consistent, and utilizes the flat ninth and flat fifth, but it is wholly dependent upon the harmonic structure for its form and dimension.

Example 17 shows that consecutive seventh chords do not follow each other in identical forms. The chord fifth is present only in every other chord, otherwise the voice leading becomes a shambles: leaping leading tones, cross relations, and misresolved sevenths are unavoidable unless common tones are held and all non-common upper voices resolved down by step.

Before proceeding it may be wise to state that Example 17 is a faithful reduction of an orchestral score. The frequent descent of the melody into the register of the accompaniment where it may reasonably be expected to be obscured is pianistically impractical but in the orchestra, where balance and clarity are achieved through the distribution of tone colors, the theme speaks clearly and with unmistakable authority. When the passage is played on the piano it is wise to sound the melody in the octave above the written pitch.

A series of chords such as illustrated in Examples 16 and 17, negating a tonal center by contradicting the resolution of a multiplicity of dominant seventh chords, creates an air of uncertainty. The bass progression of assorted perfect fourths and descending perfect fifths, the cycle of fifths, is not often bound by the conditions of key and scale. Example 16 though hardly more than an expansion of the E minor V to I progression does not, in its bass tones or chord tones, adhere to the tones of a distinct E minor scale. Example 17 is also aimed at the tonic key. It would have been a simple procedure for Brahms or Tchaikovsky to arrive at a key other than that of the point of departure. A modulation is easily effected if, during the transit of roots through the cycle of fifths, a chord of the minor third, perfect or diminished fifth and minor seventh is inserted. It will function as a II^7 and followed by V^7–I will establish a new key. Brahms, in Example 16, did not choose to modulate, but used the device to hint at relief from the constant and unvaried tonality of the movement. It is not difficult, for purposes of experiment, to modify the passage to enter the keys of D, G, C, or F major.

EXAMPLE 18

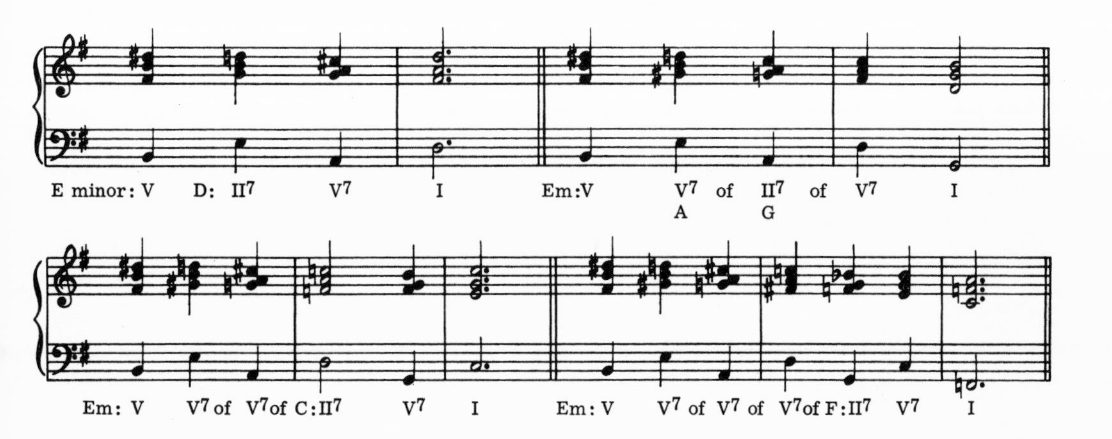

A modulation is easily accomplished by use of this device and it was often used by nineteenth-century composers. Popular music of our own era has not denied its usefulness.

The cycle of bass tones or roots moving in fifths can be found more frequently than demonstrated or implied thus far. Chords of different qualities over the bass tones, the cycle as a series of roots of inverted chords, and fragments of the cycle-series of three or four chords (as in Example 17) are seen everywhere. The procedures described in this chapter are implicit in most instances of its occurrence and are prerequisites for further expansion of the harmonic vocabulary.

V

The Chromatic Dominant Seventh Chord: Evaded Resolution

CHORD ROOTS generally tend to move down a perfect fifth: to the bass tone which would follow in dominant to tonic progression. The deceptive, or equally familiar term, evaded cadence, V^7 to VI of the diatonic repertoire, contradicts this natural tendency. Just as the deceptive cadence postpones the relaxation of tension implied by the cadential V^7, so does the upward stepwise resolution of the chromatic dominant seventh chord deflect the course of harmonic inevitability.

When the environment is not diatonic all the procedures of voice-leading applied in resolution of the diatonic V^7 to VI are simply transposed to the major or minor key implied by the chromatic dominant. The dominant is complete with root, third, fifth, and seventh. The root moves up by step, the fifth down by step, and the diminished fifth or augmented fourth between the third and seventh is resolved as usual—fourth outward and fifth inward. These rules of procedure apply when the root moves up a half-step to a major triad as in the V^7 to VI of minor keys or up a whole step to a minor triad as in the major mode. Both of these progressions are common in chromatic usage.

EXAMPLE 19. Bizet: *Carmen,* Entr'acte

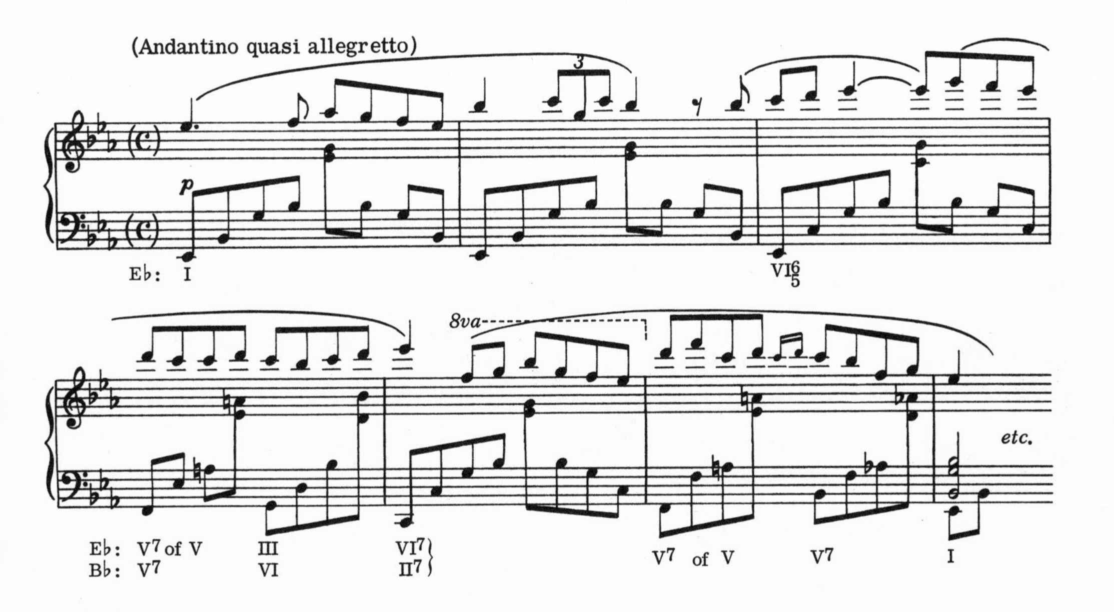

The voice-leading is not readily visible here but the root progression is clearly borrowed from the dominant key. The dominant seventh of B♭ major occurs as a deflector of tonality (measure four of the example), up a step to III, and as the dominant of the dominant (measure six) resolving as expected. Notice the presence of the cycle of fifths in the root relationships of the last five chords. After the resolution of the V^7 of V in measure four is evaded, the roots as though drawn by a magnet, go unerringly to the tonic.

The harmony of Example 19 is complete in the accompaniment. The arpeggiated texture—native to the harp which plays it—seems to be a far cry from the familiar four voice texture of choral music. Analysis shows, however, that the customary procedures of voice-leading are evident. Instrumental sonority is aided by octave doubling of chord tones. Idiomatic instrumental technic is featured in the distribution of chord tones and their occurrence in succession rather than simultaneously. Nevertheless, leading tones and chord sevenths are resolved, and the more stable chord tones move by step or short distances. Comparison of the sound and the appearance of this excerpt will be fruitful.

The next example is perhaps clearer because the chords are sounded as chords rather than arpeggios.

EXAMPLE 20. Mozart: *The Magic Flute,* Act I, Introduction

It is an incidental occurrence when viewed from the standpoint of the total operatic picture, but it shows an important and obvious resource as utilized by a master. The key signature of three flats can be ascribed to the key of the beginning of the scene, C minor. By the time this excerpt occurs the key of A flat has been established and the quotation suggests no other tonality.

The first three notes outlining the tonic chord arrive at a first inversion of the A flat major triad. C, the third of the major triad and therefore not to be doubled except in clearly contrapuntal situations, is here doubled in alto and bass because it is still the remembered tonic of C minor and hence a tonal degree.

The chromatic dominant seventh which follows flows from this I^6. It is complete with root, third, fifth, and seventh, and resolves up a step. The progression is identical to that of the V^7 to VI in the minor mode, and shows again how the transposition of diatonic progressions so often enriches, without undermining, a truly tonal environment.

VI

The Minor Mode in Major Keys

THE MAJOR MODE is a natural phenomenon and is always assumed when a single tone is heard. With the sustaining pedal depressed play a low bass tone on the piano and stretch your ears to catch a chord quality. This simple experiment will prove tonality: two undisputable facts emerge. The irrepressible tones which sound most clearly are perfect fifths and major thirds, those which complete the major triad and imply the major tonal center. The second fact is the realization that no tone is solitary: all musical sounds have, for those who depend upon their sense of hearing instead of willful adventuring, a relationship, an undeniable connection with other tones. This chapter attempts to describe one more manifestation of the interplay among the community of tones: the association of major and minor.

The minor mode is far less stable than the major because of the natural occurrence of the major third in the harmonic series. The major third in the tonic chord of a minor key (the *Tierce de Picardie*), and the fact that vast areas of compositions in minor are actually in related or even parallel major tonalities testify to the dominance of major over minor.

The colors of the minor mode are not less effective, however, and are frequently chromatically introduced into a major tonality. Subdominant chords with minor thirds and major triads on the lowered sixth scale step are often included in works in the major mode. Both these and other subtle borrowings are visible in Example 21.

EXAMPLE 21. Mascagni: *Cavalleria Rusticana,* Finale

The intensity of the operatic scene which takes place with this music is of course due to preceding dramatic events, its climactic tension and the passion of the tenor voice which sings it, but chromaticism is an important factor in the musical scene-setting.

The tonic A flat is sounded as a pedal tone through the first four measures of the quotation. Over it are heard the tonic triad, the subdominant triad of the parallel minor and the diatonic major subdominant triad. Appoggiature appear on the first beats of measures two and four. In the second measure the appoggiatura is inflected (G flat) to conform with the tonality of the *chord,* not the firmly established key. G natural, a diatonic tone, is used when the diatonic IV supports it.

The tonic $^6_4$, implying resolution to the dominant, occupies measure five and three beats of measure six. The impetuosity and suspenseful misadventures which beset this opera are reflected in the long delayed and then evaded resolution of this chord. The evasion is accomplished by another borrowed chord. Modulation to the dominant key is usual: the destination of this progression is the dominant minor. The key of E flat minor is approached through its II^7 on the fourth beat of measure six. It could just as well bring us to E flat major, but the dominant minor is perfectly suited to the manner and mood of *Cavalleria.*

The harmonic rhythm is a bit awry in the I^6_4–V^7 cadential progression in measure seven, but again the melodramatic occasion of its occurrence must be considered.

After the cadence in E flat minor (first half of measure eight) a rather remote relationship is presumed upon. This chord will be discussed more fully in a later chapter. Suffice it to say here that the VII^7 of the dominant minor of the dominant is used as an usher in the reestablishment of the tonic key. The dominant of the dominant is not a unique introducer of the I^6_4, and the leading tone to dominant function is clear.

In measure nine an opportunity to review diatonic dominant inversions is offered. Measure ten is the high point of the tenor's aria, and includes the classical operatic *fermata.* The I^6 to II^7

does not require discussion, but measures ten and eleven show how dynamically the mixture of modes can dramatize even so mundane an event as a cadence. Measure ten shows the fine delineation of significance available when minor IV chords, subdominant functioning II chords and dominant seventh qualities are thrown into close juxtaposition. It should be noted that the effect of the cross relation (F flat = F natural) is deliberate, and is acceptable because no real progression of chords is noticeable from the second to third beat, only a change of subdominant chord quality.

The final cadence is evaded: V^7 resolves to VI of the parallel minor. This dramatic progression here serves to prevent relaxation at this point of the plot.

Such intermingling of the minor with the major mode is not often seen in such profusion in so short a passage as this, but it is the source of much non-dominant chromaticism.

The reverse procedure, chords of the major tonality introduced into a prevailing minor, is not so common because, as previously stated, a series of major-related chords will easily overcome the minor flavor. The chords of the major tonality are heard as diatonic chords in a major key and the minor tonality is lost.

It is not difficult, however, to mistake certain rather unusual diatonic minor progressions for instances of true chromaticism. The three forms of the minor scale (harmonic, melodic, and natural) are attempts to preserve the more colorful characteristics of pre-major-minor tonality, and the frequent contradiction of the minor key signature when the sixth and seventh scale steps occur are nothing more than diatonic adjustments to the harmonic and melodic precedents of the sixteenth century.

Example 22 shows some of the possible harmonizations of the raised and lowered sixth and seventh scale steps. The example illustrates these tones in the upper voice, but they also occur, though less frequently, in inner parts or in bass. Good voice-leading is the guiding factor in the employment of these adjustable scale steps, and the absence of the melodic interval of the augmented second is conspicuous (except when it occurs between tones of the same chord as in Example 22 G).

EXAMPLE 22

Colorful adjuncts of the major scale, the IV, II, and VI of the parallel minor mode are important members of the diatonic-chromatic repertoire of harmonies. Their use in conjunction with otherwise wholly diatonic progressions, with chromatic dominant seventh chords, and in modulation should be investigated. If first undertaken as laboratory experiments their study will be most rewarding, for not only will their roles be better understood, but one's ability to think and hear in a multiplicity of keys will be increased.

VII

The Neapolitan Sixth

THE NEAPOLITAN SIXTH is a widely used and unmistakably recognizable chromatic subdominant. How the label came to be fixed is conjectural; its origin is lost in the haze of history.

Some four hundred years ago, when the prevailing concept of music was melodic, a Flemish composer named Clemens Non Papa (c. 1550) made use of the Neapolitan Sixth in a purely contrapuntal composition.

EXAMPLE 23. Clemens non Papa: *Vox in Rama*

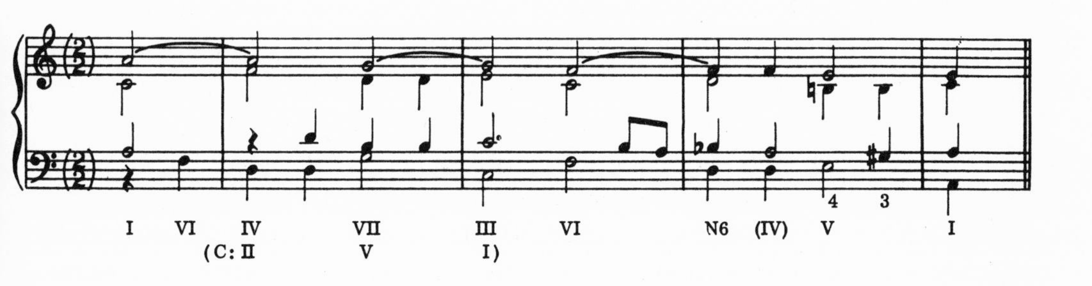

The passage quoted appears to be in A minor and we shall analyze it accordingly. The aeolian mode need not be discussed except to say that the V–I progression in C which occurs in measures one and two is not, in Renaissance practice, a departure from the key center.

The Neapolitan Sixth appears in measure three and illustrates the principles which have guided its actions through later developments. It is a triad in first inversion. Its root is the lowered second scale step, a half step above the tonic, but its bass tone is the fourth degree of the prevailing scale. The bass tone, the third of the chord and the subdominant of the key, is doubled. The resolution is to the dominant and the melodic movement of the diminished third, here B flat to G sharp, is an essential and idiomatic element of the progression. Also included among later developments are evidences that composers have been attracted by and utilized the chromatic root relationship of the Neapolitan sixth with the dominant and tonic of major keys and as IV of the submediant in minor. Root position Neapolitans and even second inversions are found in the works of many composers of the eighteenth and nineteenth centuries.

Before looking into nineteenth-century ramifications it would be wise to absorb the fact that innocuous major triads of one key may appear in chromatic garb as Neapolitan Sixths in another tonality. The familiar C major triad with third in the bass and doubled in an upper voice is the Neapolitan of C flat or B major, The G major triad similarly voiced is the Neapolitan of F sharp or G flat. This connection of remote roots is important in the development of chromatic facility. One more door to chromaticism will be opened if many diatonic triads with doubled thirds are resolved to V^7 or I^6_4 chords of the key a half step below. Stepwise motion in all voices (except the one which moves the characteristic diminished third in the resolution to the V^7) will be seen to be a crucial principle.

Robert Franz, nineteenth-century song writer of distinction, offers an example of the Neapolitan sixth chord in an arpeggiated arrangement.

EXAMPLE 24. R. Franz: *Transformation,* Op. 44 No. 3

This Example shows a cadential progression in which the subdominant is a Neapolitan (and notice the coincidence of letter names and general appearance between it and the II^6 chord), and in which the dominant resolution is evaded. The procedures of voice-leading described above are hardly visible at first glance, but if only the lowermost occurrences of the chords in measures two and three are considered their validity is readily discernible. Consider the situation from the composer's standpoint: the Neapolitan must have a doubled third, the V^7 resolving to VI must be complete in order to avoid parallel octaves, cross relations (the immediate contradiction of a chromatic or a diatonic inflection in another voice) must be avoided. Franz chose, as the lesser of two evils, to have the effect of cross relation, F natural on top in measure two, F sharp below in measure three. His solution is surely the best possible. The listener's attention is sharpened when the complete V^7 is heard, for the expectation of something unusual is suggested. The simple but exceptional resolution of the V^7 to VI combined with the preceding dynamism of the Neapolitan subdominant is enough to erase any sense of discomfort caused by the cross relation.

A more florid employment of the Neapolitan Sixth is the gist of Example 25:

EXAMPLE 25. Grieg: *Papillon,* Op. 43 No. 1

Edvard Grieg's charming portrayal of butterfly behavior incorporates the chord and its resolution as the harmonic basis for a considerable part of its duration: our quotation is representative of the manner of composition employed throughout. The two measures and one beat shown, despite the profusion of rapidly moving tones, are no more harmonically complicated than the final five beats of the sixteenth-century example quoted above. The Neapolitan of the first measure is ornamented by a descending scale passage, the final tone (F sharp) of which is a passing tone between the root of the Neapolitan and the third of the V^7. The need for this passing tone has been felt by composers of all eras: the F sharp between Grieg's G natural and E sharp, and the A between Clemens Non Papa's B flat and G sharp serve the same purpose. Such interpolations are an indication of the fact that melodic part-writing has always been a matter of concern to composers.

Measure two of Example 25 is an ornamented V^7. It is easy to name a chord for each beat but the moving voices do not produce an effect of resolution. The whole measure is dominant, and the second and third beats show a well-tried old method of enlivening sustained tones: the chord tones on the first beat are followed by their upper neighbors and the chord tones on the fourth beat are preceded by their lower neighbors. This pattern of tone succession has been variously termed *nota cambiata,* changing tone, and double neighbor notes. The choice of label is unimportant; it is important that the function, dependent upon and secondary to the harmonic basis, be recognized.

VIII

The Diminished Seventh Chord: Leading Tone Root

THE SOUND of the superimposed minor thirds of the diminished triad with diminished seventh creates an air of ambiguity, and when isolated the diminished seventh chord does not suggest a resolution with the certainty of dominant seventh chords.

EXAMPLE 26

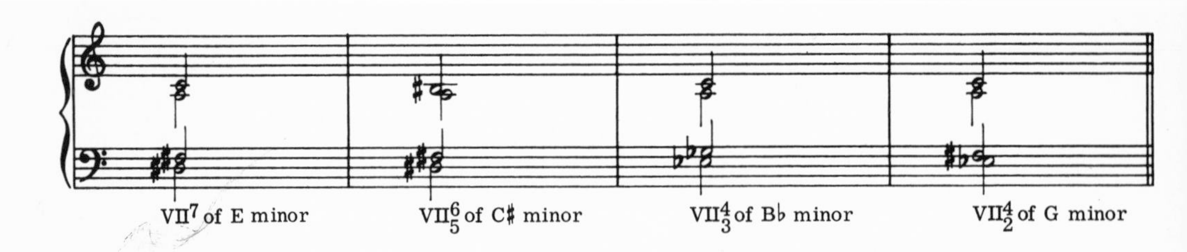

It has, nevertheless, a diatonic existence in the VII[7] of the minor mode and it is this function which is most readily transposed for chromatic use. In the world of accidentals it resolves to either major or minor triads.

Diminished and augmented intervals occur in the chord, and their resolution as intervals is difficult to evade. Although doubled thirds in root position triads are usually frowned upon in harmonic situations, the dissonant urgency of these tritones has now and then caused their resolution to take precedence over the aversion to doubled non-tonal degrees, and chromatic VII[7] to diatonic triad with doubled third is not rare.

More common, however, are instances of its use in which the composer's respect for the tonal scale steps—the transient or permanently established root, fourth and fifth scale steps—is demonstrated in the frequency with which we find doubled roots in the chords of resolution.

Felix Mendelssohn avoided the issue by writing only three voices in Example 27:

Example 27. Mendelssohn: *Scherzo,* Op. 16 No. 2

Among the points to be mentioned in the analysis of this excerpt is the occurrence of the cross relation in the first measure, G natural in the middle voice followed by G sharp in the bass. The G sharp is the bass tone of the chromatic VII[7], and this chord and all other dynamically resolution-demanding chromaticisms ride roughshod over some of the more elementary customs of voice-leading. The progression of lines to a chromatic chord are often ignored; their gentle tendencies obliterated at once by the clamorous tension of the alien harmonic intrusion. A strong tendency to move on is immediately apparent in a leap to a chromatic chord and the listener's attention is focused on future, not past events.

The G sharp on the second beat of measures one and two is the root of the VII^7 of A minor. The A minor triad is IV in the prevailing key, and in the tonic E minor the progression is simply borrowed from the subdominant tonality. The diatonic VII^7 to I is used in sequence following the chromatic use of the progression, and a familiar cadence formula ends the quotation.

Another example, this time consisting of four arpeggiated voices, is seen in Example 28; the introduction to a song for voice and piano by Camille Saint-Saens.

EXAMPLE 28. Saint-Saens: *Ave Maria*

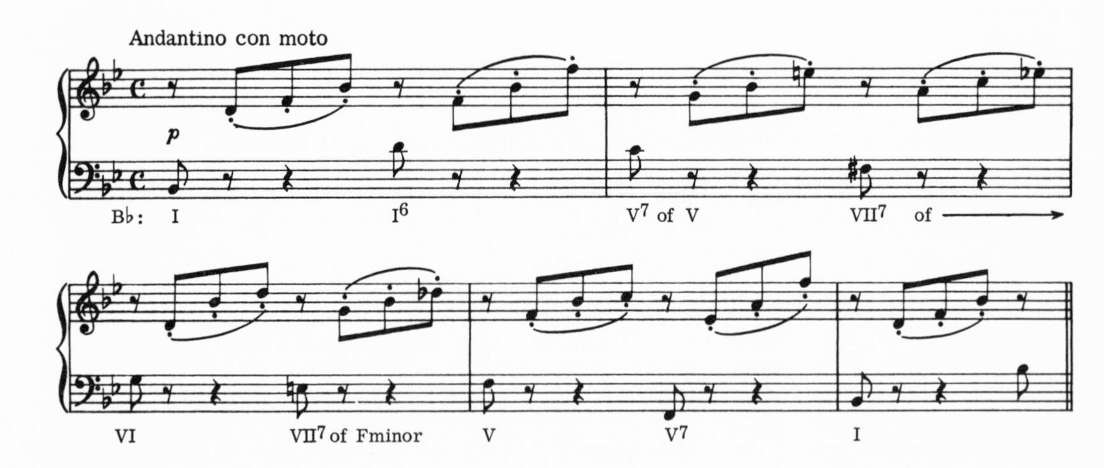

In the second measure the chromatic dominant seventh chord of the dominant key is followed by a diminished seventh chord instead of the expected dominant. Three of the tones, (A, C, and E flat) of the diminished seventh chord are members of the true dominant seventh chord of the key which might have replaced it if consecutive dominants were used. The resolution of the augmented fourth (B flat = E natural) requires discussion, for it contradicts the tendencies described in Chapter IV. The E natural moving to E flat is not exceptional: leading tones resolving down a half step to dominant quality chord sevenths are usual in consecutive dominants. B flat, the chord seventh, resolving up to C is *not* usual and can be explained only with reference to the whole chord. In a normal resolution the B flat would resolve to A and the G would resolve to the doubled root F. Here the F does not occur, but is replaced by F sharp, a chromatic tone and the leading tone of the key of the chord which follows. Leading tones in particular and chromatic tones in general are not usually doubled, and the composer here chose to depend upon the unexpectedness of the diminished quality to dispel any expectation of resolution. The pattern of the arpeggio is preserved and the startling bass leap from C to F sharp, the chromatic scale of the upper voice and the change of polarity proclaimed by the diminished seventh chord quality combine to erase all desire for resolution of V^7 of V.

Preservation of the texture—the pianistic adaptation of the chords to the arpeggio—is a factor in the resolution of this diminished seventh chord. Again we must consider the alternatives. If the third of the VI chord on the first beat of measure three is doubled as implied by the rule for resolving diminished fifths the pattern would be broken, and the pianist would be required to play two B flats instead of the written D to B flat. This repeated tone (the octave leap would be grotesque) can not be executed with the same effect of semilegato heard in the preceding and following harmonies, for the hand position as well as the pattern of tone sequence is disrupted. If the root is doubled the pattern is not disturbed, but the disturbing effect of the two tones of the diminished fifth (A to E flat) resolving without change of direction to the perfect fifth (G-D) will be felt. Saint-Saens doubles the fifth: the pianist's hand is not discomfited and, because the arpeggio figuration sounds the tones in succession rather than simultaneously, theoreticians are not unduly aggravated by the doubled fifth.

The next harmonic event is the VII^7 of V and its resolution to V. The first noticeable feature is the movement of the diminished fifth (G to D flat) to the perfect fifth (F to C). This resolution, for the avoidance of which emergency measures were taken in the preceding identical situation, is acceptable here because of the presence of the dissonant B flat which, despite its occurrence as part of the arpeggio, is a suspension. Such non-harmonic tones color the sound to a degree which distracts the attention from more consonant harmonic members, even when they result from a mildly uncontrapuntal movement.

Leading-tone diminished seventh chords (this is a conveniently descriptive label which the authors have been unable to avoid in conversation) are similar to chromatic dominants in that they resemble the V^7 to VI progression of diatonic practice. The difference between the two is the intensity gained by the substitution of the leading-tone of the key of VI for the root of the V^7.

Their source in the minor mode (VII^7 to I) may be compared to the source of a great river: it is less prepossessing than its development. Diminished sevenths occur far more frequently in chromatic music than in diatonic music and they resolve as often to major triads as to minor triads.

Because of this derivation from the VII^7 of the minor mode chromatic leading tone diminished seventh chords are theoretically invertible as any other seventh chord. First inversions are probably more frequently seen than the $^4_3$ or $^4_2$ positions, but the student should experiment with the resolution of this chord in all its arrangements. The effects of the various possible resolutions and their combination with non-harmonic tones should be evaluated.

Before proceeding to another aspect of chromaticism it should be mentioned that the function of any chromatic seventh chord may be fulfilled by a chromatic triad. A chromatic major triad may be used instead of a chromatic dominant seventh chord, and a chromatic VII^6 may occur in place of a chromatic VII$^6_5$. They provide a milder but, because of their chromatic tones, unmistakable demand for motion. They are also the simplest and clearest examples of the essentially diatonic character of the chromaticism thus far examined.

IX

The Chromatic Half-Diminished Seventh Chord

THE VII^7 of the major mode is less flexible than any other diatonic chord. Its unique structure—the leading tone root, the diminished fifth between root and fifth and perfect fifth between third and seventh—creates a certain top-heavy instability which has led many theorists to deny its existence as an independent chord. Its usual diatonic roles are shown in Example 29.

EXAMPLE 29

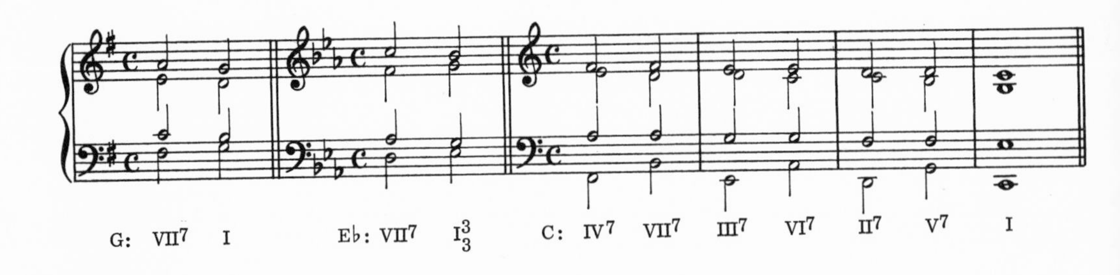

It resolves to the root position tonic triad, the third of which is doubled if the perfect fifth (third to seventh) appears between two upper voices. It may also occur, as shown, in an extended series of diatonic seventh chords resolving down a fifth or up a fourth.

The II^7 of the minor mode, identical in intervalic structure and in sound, has a different function. It resolves as II, usually to a diatonic or chromatic V, and is equally at home in either the major or minor mode. The chromatic VII^7 of the major mode is distinguishable from the chromatic II^7 of minor only by the presence of the root as leading tone to the root of the chord which follows. Because of the unmistakable identification with the major mode (the chord contains the diatonic major sixth scale step, ruling out any possibility of minor), the chord of resolution is always major: usually dominant, occasionally subdominant.

EXAMPLE 30. Franck: Symphony in D Minor, First movement

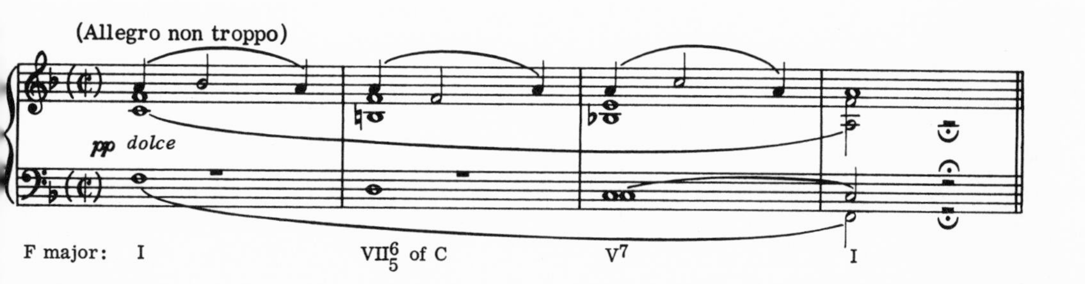

Measures 175 to 178 of the first movement of César Franck's only symphony are quoted in Example 30. The chromatic half-diminished VII^6_5 in the second measure clearly shows why the chord has been called a dominant ninth without the root. The resolutions of F, B natural, and D are exactly as they would be if G were in the bass and the progression was V^7 of V to V^7. However, G is *not* present, and the sound of the passage is drastically changed if it is added, either above or below the D. It is difficult to justify the existence of a chord whose root is inadmissible! The four measure phrase quoted in Example 30 occurs nine times during the course of the movement, in four different keys and scored for various instrumental combinations and in various densities of texture. The one constant feature is the harmonic progression (the melody sometimes continues its motion during and past the measure which here has the *fermata*), and at no time does the composer infer that the VII$^6_5$ is a representative of something else.

The non-harmonic tones in the melody may be mentioned. The B flat in measure one is an upper neighbor. The A in measure three may be described as a suspension which resolves as a common tone in the following I chord, or simply as a tone of the dominant thirteenth chord.

Another undeniable chromatic half-diminished VII^7 is seen in Example 31, the last six measures of a song for tenor or soprano voice by Sergei Rachmaninoff.

EXAMPLE 31. Rachmaninoff: *Lilacs*, Op. 21 No. 5

(Allegretto)

I V$^4_2$ of IV VI 6 V$^4_2$ of IV

VI VII^7 of E♭ A♭: I$^6_4$ V^7

The key of A flat has been clearly established in the measures which precede the quotation and the low bass A flat sounded in measures one and two preserves the tonality in spite of the rather vague harmonies above. The alternating dominant seventh chord of D flat and F minor triad suggest the region of the subdominant without establishing it. The intricate appearing treble staff of the piano part is made up entirely of chord tones except for one pitch. A flat and C are members of every chord from the beginning of the quotation to the arrival of the V^7 at the end of measure four and B flat is regularly inserted as a passing tone between these two chord tones.

The VI chord in measure three, acceptable as II of E flat, resolves to the VII^7 of E flat major, wrenching the tonality from the subdominant to the dominant region. The appoggiatura (G) in the voice is doubled in the piano as are its resolution and the following accented chromatic passing tone (F flat) and its resolution to the consonant E flat.

The occurrence of the tone C over the dominant seventh chord in the concluding measures is another instance of the placid third of the I chord being retained or introduced over the dominant as a thirteenth. A non-harmonic definition is not difficult to find, but the frequency with which it is found as in these two examples suggests that it be recognized as a chord tone.

The resolution of the chromatic half-diminished VII^7 rarely differs from the procedures shown in Examples 30 and 31, although it may be used as a modulatory chord to enter another key. The bare harmonies of a few possible modulating progressions utilizing the chromatic half-diminished VII^7 are given in Example 32.

EXAMPLE 32

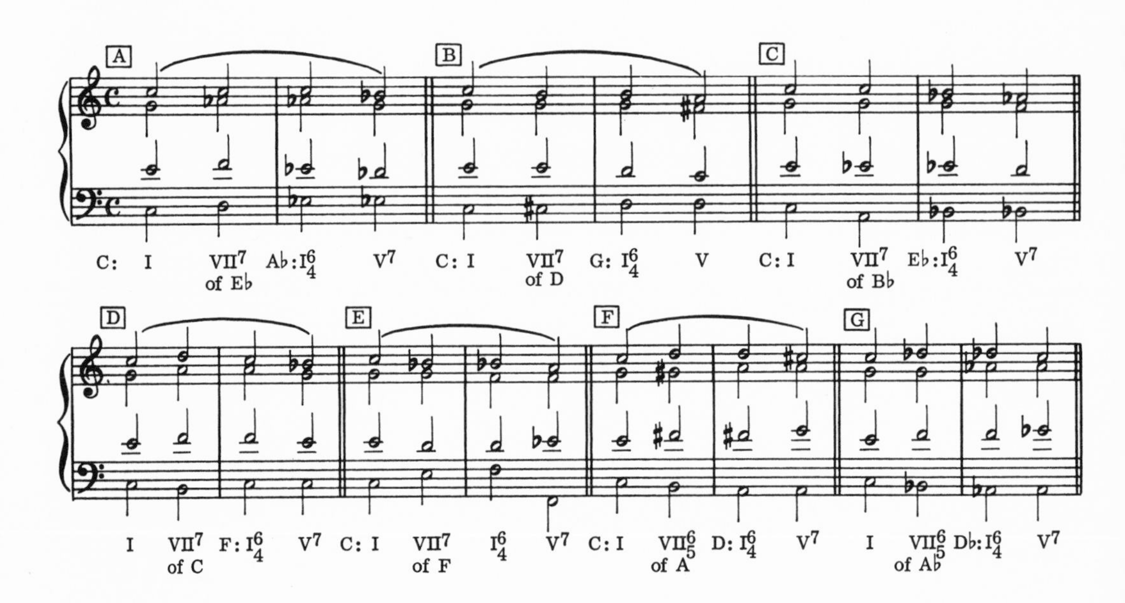

This chord, in its resolution, may be the most restricted of chromaticisms but it is by no means the least effective. Composers have used it with restraint, taste, and discretion: students are advised to listen to it in context; analyze and compare its effect with that of other chords, such as complete chromatic dominant ninths. The authors are confident that the chord will then prove itself to be real and complete—not a sound which requires an additional tone to prove its existence.

X

The Diminished Seventh Chord: Evaded Resolution

CHAPTER VIII, which dealt with the literal transposition of the minor mode VII^7 into nondiatonic environments showed only one facet of the role of this chord in chromatic harmony. No other chromatic chord is so taken for granted by casual musicians, or so widely misunderstood. No other chromatic chord is so immediately available for the easing of strain in the connection of relatively remote chords; as harmonic support for melodic tones, which without them would be non-harmonic; and for the addition of chromaticism to simple diatonic relationships. Example 33 is a simplified illustration of these three functions: C major to F sharp minor; diminished sevenths used to harmonize non-harmonic tones; and I^6 to IV to I^6.

EXAMPLE 33

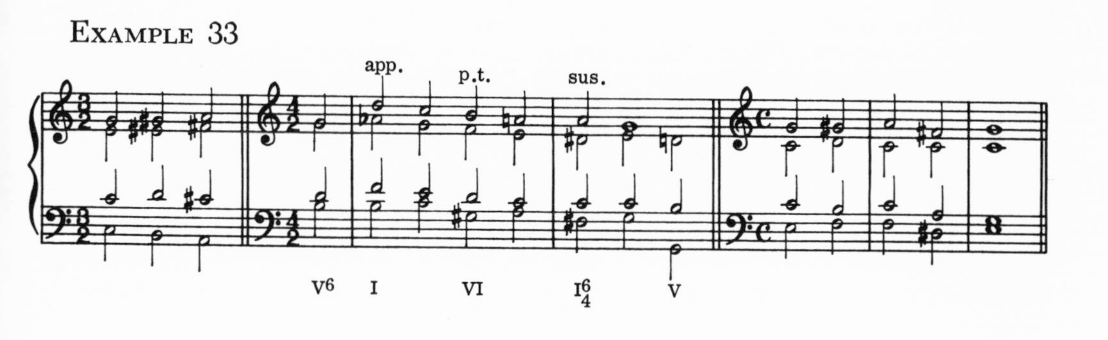

The evaded resolution of the diminished seventh chord is seen only in the third of these three samples; the first two illustrating the now familiar resolution of the VII^7 of the minor mode to the major or minor chord a half step above.

A conspicuous feature of the evaded resolution is the common tone between a tone of the diminished seventh and the root of the chord to which it resolves. The diatonic source of the progression is seen in Example 34. Just as the V^7 may resolve to VI instead of I, the VII^7 (inverted or in root position) may resolve to the triad or seventh chord whose root is VI of the key in which the VII^7 occurs diatonically.

EXAMPLE 34

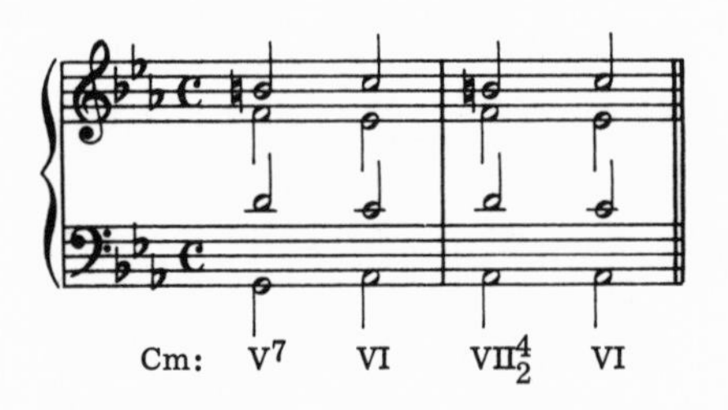

This resolution is used chromatically in Example 35, which shows the chord in each of its inverted positions. The voice leading should be noticed: each chromatic tone is spelled and resolved as a leading-tone to the *individual tone* to which it resolves, without reference to the prevailing tonality or chord quality.

EXAMPLE 35

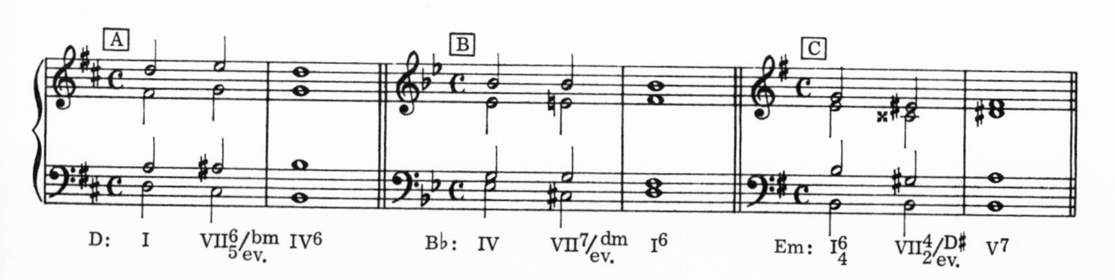

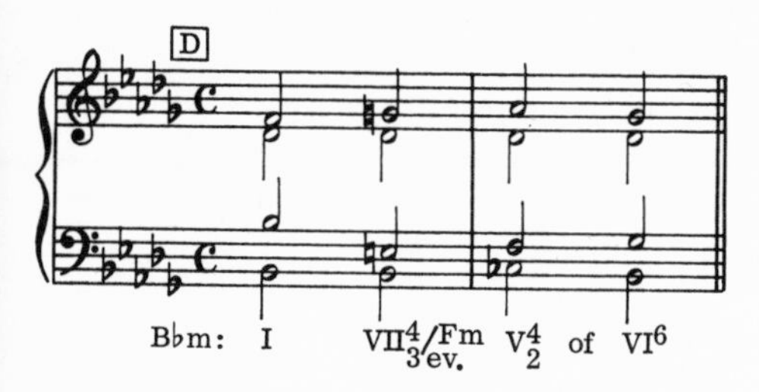

Exceptions to this principle of leading-tone resolution are less frequent than they appear to be. At first glance the A flat to A natural in Example 36 would seem to be exceptional, and the G sharp to A correct. Composers, however, often consider that a chord of resolution should be a true resolution and not an intermediate or delaying one.

EXAMPLE 36

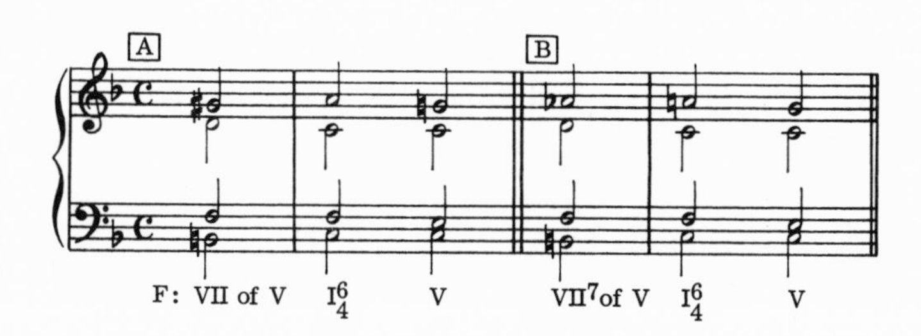

G sharp to A is correct only if the following six-four chord is considered the essential chord of resolution. A flat to A is more logical if it is realized that the root-position C chord is the real destination of the diminished seventh, and the six-four chord is essentially non-harmonic. The progression will then be seen to be of the leading-tone-root variety (Chapter VIII) and not evaded, for the leading tone is B, not G sharp.

Resolutions other than those described are rare and usually unsuccessful. The diminished seventh chord, without a perfect fifth and with its four tones equidistant from each other, easily loses its identity when not clearly a VII^7 resolving to a I or to a VI. Example 37 summarizes a not uncommon procedure.

EXAMPLE 37

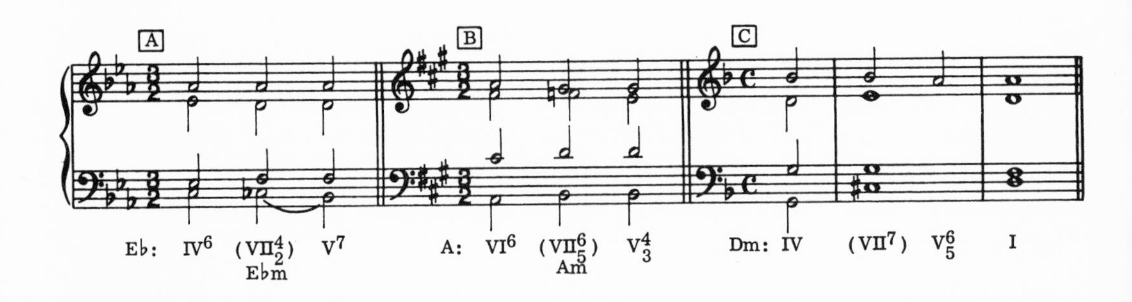

The diminished sevenths, with three tones in common with the dominant seventh chords which follow them, are submerged by the strength of the dominant quality. The C flat between C and B flat and the F natural between F sharp and E tend to sound like passing tones, and the B flat in the third progression is readily accepted by the ear as a suspension. The reason of course is that both the VII^7 and the V^7 tend toward the tonic, the V^7 much more specifically. Once the dominant seventh quality is heard all immediately preceding lesser dominant forms (V triad, VII^6, VII^7) tend to be remembered as parts of the V^7 rather than independent harmonic units.

Evaded resolutions occur in Examples 38 and 39. Rimsky-Korsakov demonstrates an important point: the use of non-harmonic tones over the diminished seventh chord.

EXAMPLE 38. Rimsky-Korsakov: *Capriccio Espagnol*

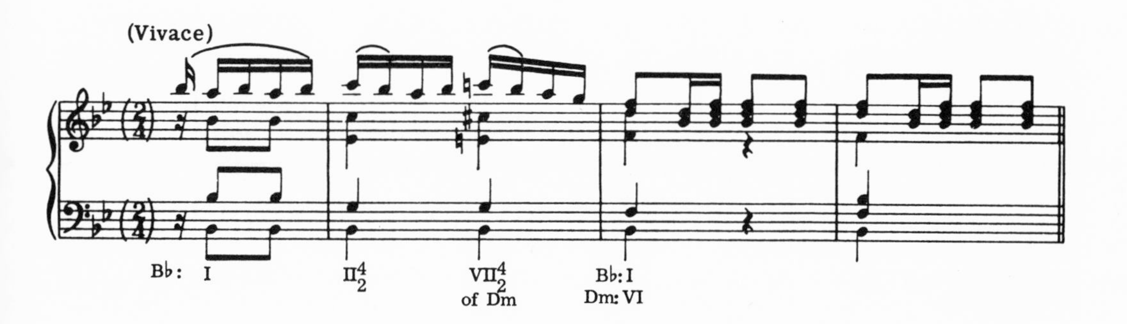

The C natural and A are non-harmonic, not because they are natural diatonic tones in the key, but because they are a whole-step above and a half-step below chord tones. If the VII^4_2 were continued one more beat and the descending scale continued for four more sixteenth notes the tones would be F sharp, E natural, D sharp, C sharp: any other accidentals would disrupt and obscure the diminished seventh quality of the chord.

The short quotation from Franz Liszt's A Major Piano Concerto also relates to non-harmonic tones.

EXAMPLE 39. Liszt: Piano Concerto No. 2

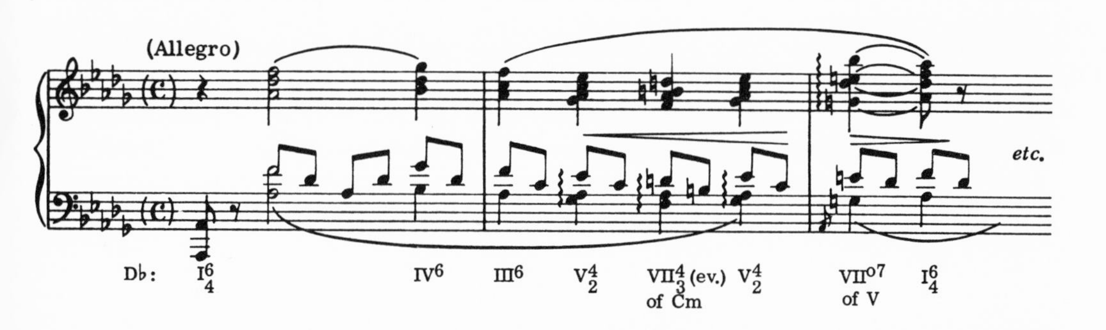

The D natural in measure two is a simple melodic lower neighbor note which could occur over the dominant seventh chord. The B flat on the first beat of the final measure is an obvious appoggiatura and could just as well occur over the tonic chord. The passage illustrates the use of diminished sevenths to give this non-harmonic flavor to the whole texture rather than to the melody only.

Other points to be noted are the implied pedal point and the deflected resolution of the dominant $^4_2$. The isolated low A flats at the beginning of the quotation and on the first beat of the last measure are enough to give the whole passage an atmosphere of I^6_4—a suspended and unsettled feeling. This condition has an important bearing on the unusual resolution of the V^4_2 on the fourth beat of the second measure. Because of the implied bass A flat, the G flat is not really the bass tone, but is only the result of the doubling of the melody and the inner parts in the left hand an octave below the right. It is also not unusual for a chord seventh to be deflected a half-step upward when the change of direction is brought about by the interjection of an actively dissonant chromaticism, as here.

The effect of the inversions, the voice-leading and the diatonic surroundings of the diminished sevenths of Examples 38 and 39 should be compared with Example 35. Other uses of the diminished seventh should be sought—and analyzed when found. The chord which is the subject of this discussion presents a highly chromatic appearance in many and various spellings and a wide diversity of styles and situations. It is not the easiest of chromatic chords to understand. Its structure is simple; its functions are not. Although wholly diatonic in origin its frequency and diversity of use in chromatic music far exceed its diatonic use, and its study is thus a large step closer to chromaticism which is more than transposed diatonic harmony.

XI

Non-Harmonic Tones, Modulation, and Harmonic Rhythm in Chromatic Music

BEFORE PROCEEDING to the examination of further manifestations of chromaticism it will be well to digress a bit. Non-harmonic tones, modulation, and harmonic rhythm are as vital a part of chromatic music as of diatonic music. The following discussion will, quite briefly, deal with each in turn.

NON-HARMONIC TONES

In diatonic practice a non-harmonic tone should be a tone which, when sounded with the supporting harmony, proves its non-harmonic role by sounding a pitch dissonant enough to prove that it cannot possibly be heard as part of a recognizable chord. In chromatic usage this rule remains in effect but with considerably less authority. In an environment in which any tone (sharp, flat, or natural) is a recognizable member of the community, the relative dissonance, chord membership or non-membership, is not as easily defined. Events such as those shown in Example 40 are not hard to find and those of us who feel obliged to write meaningful figured bass symbols beneath the lowest tone are often troubled by them.

EXAMPLE 40

An over-detailed harmonic analysis becomes superfluous if the impetus toward resolution is strongly felt in visually ambiguous situations. In sound the function of the complex of tones is more important than a definition of vertical coincidences of pitch. Example 40 is best described in terms of *function* rather than *chord labels.* It is basically no more than the progression of I to V of II to II. The passing tone (B) between the A of the I chord and the C sharp which follows is easily recognized, but the six beats of alternating C sharp and B sharp pose a question. The clarity of sound can be obscured in a cloud of theoretical terminology such as: "the VII^7 chords of E major and E minor are interchanged with each other; the VII^7 of E minor is enharmonically spelled because its seventh acts as the lower neighbor to the chord seventh of the VII^7 of E major, but when the chord of resolution (the II chord) is arrived at, the seventh of the VII^7 of E minor is enharmonically altered to C natural, the true sixth step of the E minor scale, and becomes the root of the VI chord of E minor in the evaded resolution of the diminished seventh chord." Such an explanation is purely the result of looking, not listening. In sound, the only valid basis for evaluation, the passage is simply a I to II progression accomplished by means of a leading tone seventh chord to the II ornamented with neighbor notes and a suspension.

EXAMPLE 41

Example 41 could be mistakenly described as (one chord per melodic tone) I, VI^6, VII^7 (inc.) of II, B minor triad (!), A♭ major triad in first inversion, diminished $^4_3$ (inc.) of VI, II, II$^6_5$, VII$^6_4$, III^7, I^6. The discerning listener will recognize the non-harmonic melodic tones—the F sharp in measure one, the A flat and F sharp in measure two (these three tones act as double neighbors), the B flat on the third beat of measure two, and the C in measure three. The harmonic progression then is heard as I, VII^7 of II, II, VII$^6_4$, I^6.

Diatonic progressions can also pose alternative possibilities. There are only two questions prompted by Example 42: how to define the chords on the first downbeat and the downbeat of measure three?

EXAMPLE 42

The appearance of these harmonic entities is so authoritatively in keeping with their surroundings that the temptation to name them as chords is strong. Many a theorist will aver that the progression shown is IV, III^6, V^7, VI, IV, V^{11}, V^7, I. Others will deny only the V^{11} because they are reasonably convinced that the term V^{11} declares the presence or admissibility of the root, third, fifth, seventh, ninth, and eleventh. The third of the chord is utterly foreign to its function and the harmony is therefore not definable as an eleventh chord, but is here clearly non-harmonic: the A and F sharp are suspensions, and for identification completely dependent upon their resolution. The III^6 may also be explained as a non-harmonic occurrence. C sharp is an accented passing tone, E is the doubled root acting as a passing tone between F sharp and D in order to avoid the classically forbidden unprepared harmonic dissonance. If the III^6 were to resolve directly to the VI chord, the V^7 being omitted, there would be no debate. The urgency and unmistakable conviction of the dominant seventh chord makes its purpose clear in both directions. Once heard, its immediate predecessor is remembered as either its introducer or as a disguised form of itself, a chord of either subdominant or dominant function. The III is in some circles called a substitute for the V, but in a circumstance such as that illustrated its disguise fails and we see through it.

How true it is that harmony can be understood only after melody is understood! All the chords, chromatic and diatonic, and all the non-harmonic tones which appear in our study are the result of melody—the fundamental motivation of music. Chords are only supporters of melody: non-harmonic tones are proof that melody retains its freedom.

MODULATION

A new tonal center is established by time: any tone can be made I if its tonality is insisted upon long enough. Modulation is a term which implies the process of destroying the authority of one tonic and establishing the authority of another. Each of the chords thus far described as chromatic (except the Neapolitan sixth) has at least one diatonic existence. Each may be the means by which the key in which it occurs chromatically is left and the key of its diatonic origin entered. The chromatic V7 or VII♭7 of II, for instance, may resolve to II and be followed by a series of chords which are wholly concerned with the key of II, and a modulation will thus have been effected. When the possible resolutions of all the chromatic chords are considered it will be seen that even modulation to remote keys is a simple matter: remember that the Neapolitan Sixth is a major triad, and major triads occur as I, IV, and V of major keys and III, V, and VI of minor keys. Refer again to Example 18, pg. 41; Example 32, pg. 66.

Many an excursion into a non-tonic tonality takes place and proves to be too brief to be called a modulation. Such digression into a recognizable key, lacking both a cadence and enough duration to establish the tonality, are best termed *regions.*

Example 43. Handel: *Sarabande*

George Frederick Handel, in Example 43, departs from the tonality of D minor only long enough to state the I and V chords of F major. The implied chromatic VII^6 of IV is used to re-enter the key of D minor and its resolution to IV begins the progression IV, I, IV^6, V, and the phrase ends with a half-cadence. It is unrealistic to name the F major chord as a major III of D minor and the C major chord a flat VII triad. It is equally unrealistic to consider that modulations from D minor to F major and F major to D minor have taken place. No one who listens could possibly forget the tonality of D so quickly and on the basis of only two chords and no cadence.

Also worthy of notice in this example are the non-harmonic tones. The quarter notes in measures one, three, five, and seven are beautifully clear specimens of the *échappée*. The upper neighbor note (B flat) in measure two, the passing tones in measures two, four, and six (all quarter notes), and the suspension (A) in measure seven are equally straightforward representatives of their kind.

HARMONIC RHYTHM

An awareness of harmonic rhythm, the relative duration of chords and their motion as compared to the prevailing meter, is important only when there is danger of an unwarranted repetition of bass tones over bar lines, wrongly emphasized six-four chords, or bizarre and confusing irregularities of root movement. All these are diatonic considerations. In an attempt to apply a preconceived theory of harmonic motion to chromatic music great allowances must be made for the diversity of functions performed by chromatic chords. They may assume the role of essential members of a chord progression. They may only intensify, diminish, or obscure the function of a preceding or following chord. They may be inserted in an otherwise stable progression simply for dramatic effect, and finally, they may be used to harmonize non-harmonic melodic tones of relatively short duration. Each of these aspects of chromatic usage can be seen in the short excerpts quoted in the preceding and following chapters. Example 44 is an attempt to show each of these functions as applied to a simple diatonic progression.

EXAMPLE 44

Compare (a) and (b): The chromatic V^4_3 of II replaces the I^6, assuming its role as an essential harmonic member of the progression. In (c) the V^4_3 of II follows the I^6 clarifying the role of measure two as the introduction of the II chord. Motion in the inner voices is added in (d), and appears to form a chord on each beat. The essential function of the measure remains unchanged. A suspension is added in (e), and harmonized with a diminished seventh chord, VII^6_5 of II.

The harmonic rhythm of each of these versions of the progression appears to be different from each of the others. The moral of all this would seem to be: the true function of any chord can be determined only with reference to its tonal associations. Its duration or metrical position are not indicative of any significant factor unless this tonal association is first understood.

XII

The Augmented Sixth Chords: The Italian Sixth

IT WILL HAVE been observed that the most frequently used chromatic tone is the raised fourth scale step, the leading tone of the dominant key. When relief from the diatonic environment is desired the first way to gain it is by this reference to its most nearly related tonality. Just as the dominant side of the diatonic is suggested by the raised fourth degree, the subdominant side is chromatically represented by the lowered sixth scale step. The chromatic minor IV chord and the V^7 of V are so familiar that they hardly seem foreign to the diatonic vocabulary; especially at cadences where they serve only to reinforce the tonality.

EXAMPLE 45

Long ago, no one knows when or where, the two chromatic tones of Example 45 became associated with each other, combining to intensify the function, previously served by each individually, of adding a dash of the chromatic to an otherwise routine coming together of closely related tones.

The interval between these two tones is an augmented sixth. Its inevitable tendency to resolve to the doubled dominant has been felt by composers so strongly that the interval has given rise to a family of chords, oddly bearing national names, with the resolution of the augmented sixth in common.

The first of these is the Italian Sixth. It is first because it is the simplest: it consists of only the augmented sixth and the tonic note.

Example 46

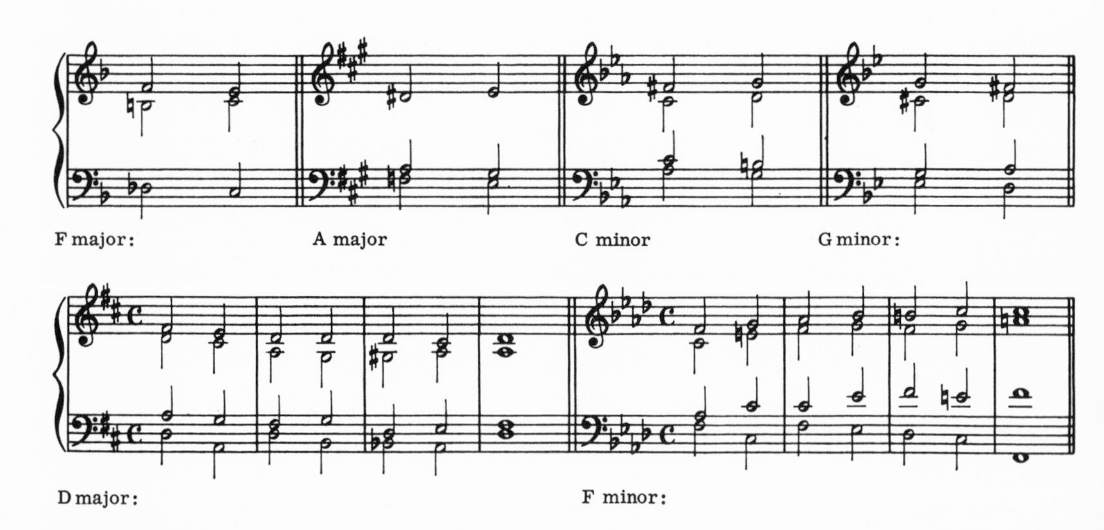

The Italian Sixth is a three-voice chord: the third above the bass tone (the tonic of the key) is doubled when four voices take part. Because of the very strong tendency toward and emphasis upon the dominant, augmented sixth chords never fail to suggest the imminence of a cadence. The Italian Sixth resolves directly to the dominant triad, seldom to the I^6_4 or V^7. Any dissonance in the chord of resolution must be non-harmonic, and the only non-harmonic tone seen with any frequency is the suspension of one of the doubled tones in its resolution to the third of the V chord. Example 47 (a) shows this device.

EXAMPLE 47

The suspension occurs in (b) also, and when resolved is accompanied by the addition of the seventh of the dominant triad. This arrangement, with the doubled root descending through the seventh as a passing tone, results in a final I chord with tripled root. A better deployment of tones is seen in (c). Here the seventh occurs in the voice which sounds the fifth of the V chord. The seventh is approached through an accented passing tone. The passing tone could have been unaccented or omitted as in Example 48.

EXAMPLE 48

After these principles of the Italian Sixth behavior are thoroughly absorbed another facet of its usefulness may be looked into.

The interval of the augmented sixth is, in sound, indistinguishable from the interval of the minor seventh. The two intervals differ only in function and notation. The minor seventh is assumed when no indication of something else is present. The diatonic minor seventh and its transposition are so common that the augmented sixth, which has no diatonic existence, is always a surprise. Composers have used this coincidence of sound in modulation. Giacomo Rossini, prolific writer of Italian operas, used the Italian sixth to make a quick change of tonal center in Example 49.

EXAMPLE 49. Rossini: *Bianca e Falerio*, "Cavatina"

The piece is in the key of A major, but before the quoted excerpt occurs the key of C major has been clearly established and is in effect at the beginning of this example. Measure one consists of I and V^6_5 of C. Measure two begins as I, the resolution of the V^6_5, but the upper voice of the accompaniment rises chromatically through the raised fifth (a chromatic passing tone as used here but forming a triad of augmented quality), the sixth (which may be considered, since it is preceded by its own leading tone, to be the root of the VI chord of C), to the augmented sixth above the bass tone. When the augmented sixth is heard its function is not clear; it could be the minor seventh over C leading to the IV chord of C or it could be an upper neighbor of A about to descend through the same series of tones by which it ascended. It could also be, and is, the Italian Sixth of the key of E, the dominant of the key of the piece. When the A sharp and the C natural resolve to the doubled B the tonal center is irrevocably changed, for the doubled leading tone of C approached through its own leading tone and the D sharp (which cannot possibly be heard as an enharmonic E flat, the lowered third of C) positively proclaim a departure from the established key. The composer having disrupted the key in so drastic a manner retards the cadential formula in E major and allows the vocalist, restricted to chord tones in the C major portion of the excerpt, time to show a bit of *coloratura* while we adjust to the new tonality. The realization that this too is only a fragment of a complete composition is brought home to us by the last measure. V^7 of E resolves to VI, and no sense of finality results. If this lack of relaxation is found unacceptable the student is advised to study the complete work. The authors did, and found it worth the effort.

XIII

The German Sixth

THE SECOND augmented sixth chord to be discussed is hardly more than a completed Italian Sixth. Its distinguishing feature is one which in the vast majority of other chords is so commonplace that it is almost neutral in effect: the perfect fifth above the bass tone. The German Sixth is an Italian Sixth with the added perfect fifth or, identical in sound, doubly augmented fourth. The notation of the interval is governed by its environment: the perfect fifth is seen in Example 50, and the doubly augmented fourth in Example 51.

EXAMPLE 50. Bruch: Violin Concerto, Op. 26, First movement

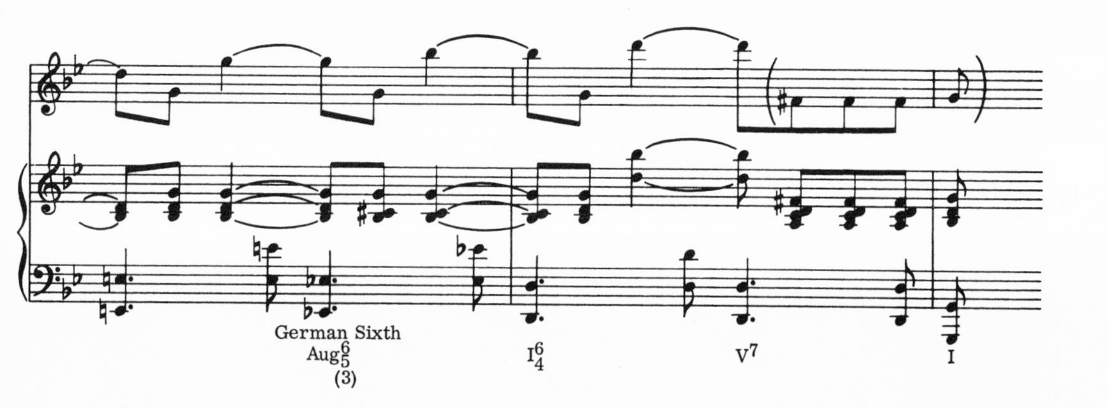

Example 50 is presented in a three line score in order to separate the harmonic function from the melodic elaborations of the upper voice. The upper staff is superimposed over the lower two, which by themselves show the harmonic structure.

The bass line illustrates a frequently met with idiomatic procedure. In the descending minor scale the raised leading tone (F sharp in this key) is not used because of its upward tendency. E natural is a chromatic passing tone to E flat, the diatonic sixth scale step. The motion during the first two and one-half measures of the quotation is thus non-harmonic, and the stability of the tonic triad is undisturbed except for the implication of motion to come as indicated by the bass.

The German Sixth intensifies the tonality, for the augmented sixth (C sharp) is the leading tone to the dominant and the bass tone is the sixth step of the scale. Both these tones leave no doubt as to their destination; their function is exactly as in the resolution of the Italian Sixth (and the yet to be discussed French Sixth). The third above the bass tone is repeated as a common tone, as in Example 47 (a and b) it was suspended as the fourth above the dominant, delaying its resolution to the third of the V^7.

The fifth above the bass tone is also retained as a common tone in the resolution to the I^6_4. This is the essential point of difference between the resolutions of the Italian and German Sixth chords. The Italian Sixth normally resolves to the dominant triad. The natural destination of the German Sixth chord is the cadential I^6_4.

At the cadence the upper part joins the harmonic voices after having spread the tones of the tonic triad over an octave and a half (the A in measures one and two is an upper neighbor and seems to be "winding up" in preparation for the leaps).

The famous "Sextette from Lucia" provides another instance of use of the German Sixth.

EXAMPLE 51. Donizetti: *Lucia di Lammermoor,* "Sextette"

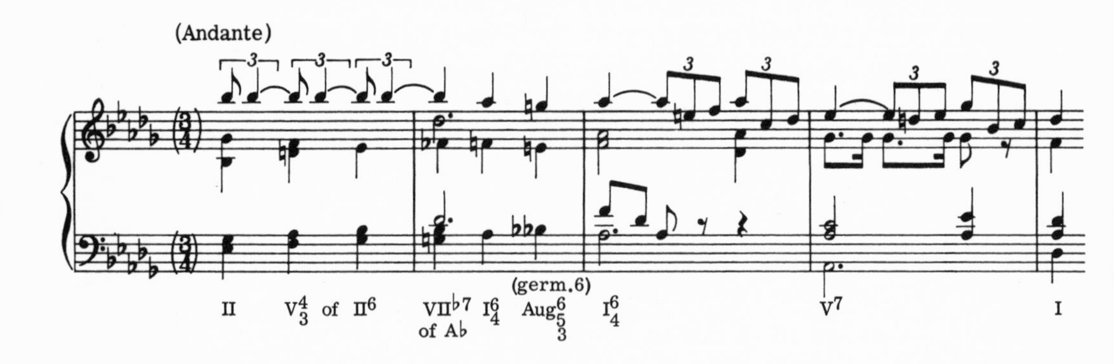

Six part voice-leading with a vocabulary of three and four tone chords is not a very practical undertaking for any but the most highly skilled in counterpoint, and this Donizetti was not. Our attempt to compress this fragment of the piece into two staves does not convey the effect of the six participants, each an individually important and well defined operatic character. It may not be clear enough for present purposes and its harmonic structure is shown in a four part reduction in Example 52:

EXAMPLE 52

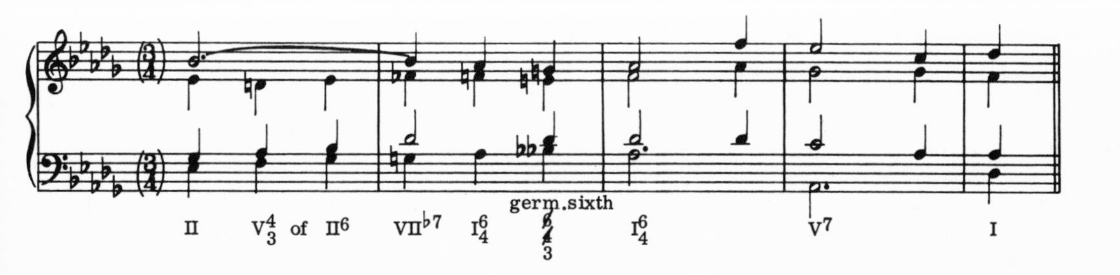

Measure one shows an inverted chromatic dominant as described in Chapter III. The first chord in the second measure is a diminished seventh chord which could have been spelled another way as seen in Chapter X, Example 36 (a and b). It resolves to the I^6_4 on the second beat but only in anticipation of its far more dynamic appearance in the following measure. The bass line and chords of measure two serve to emphasize the arrival of the cadential I^6_4 in its rhythmically accented position on the first beat of measure three. The German Sixth precedes it, and the perfect fifth above the bass tone is spelled as a doubly augmented fourth because it here functions as a leading tone to the third of the I^6_4. This condition occurs in major keys. In minor keys the fifth is a common tone (Example 50). Composers, aware of the inevitability of perfect fifths above bass tones and of the eventual destination (the fifth of the dominant) of the fifth of the German Sixth, frequently write the tone as a perfect fifth above the bass in major as well as in minor.

Although its natural resolution is to the tonic six-four chord an occasional German Sixth will go directly to the dominant triad.

EXAMPLE 53.

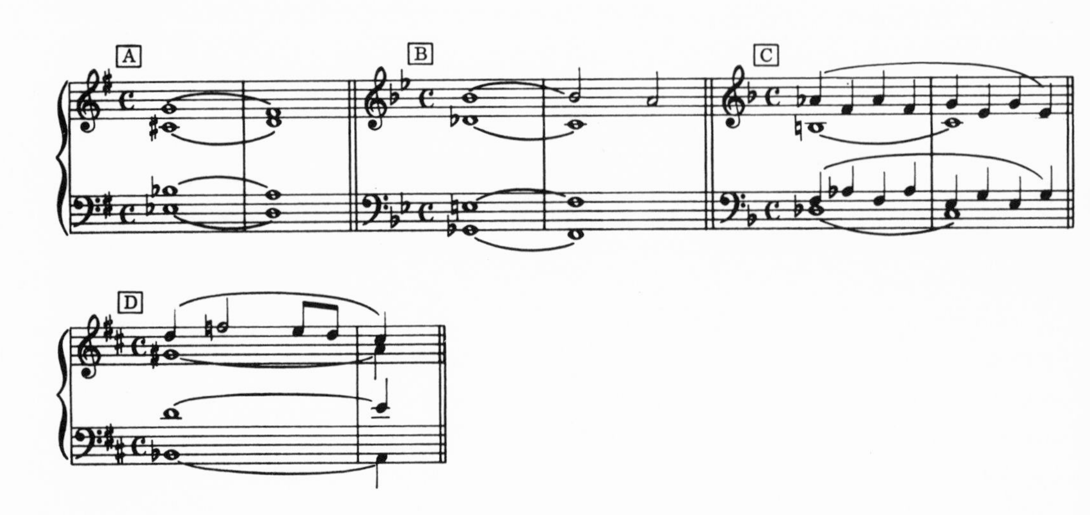

Example 53 (a) shows the inevitable and objectionable parallel perfect fifths which occur when a clear four voice arrangement is adopted. Such an arrangement is extremely rare, for composers of tonal music have shown a very practical and deep aversion for parallel fifths. In the rare moments when this aversion could be overpowered by other considerations its influence remained. First and foremost the fifths are never permitted to occur between the uppermost and lowermost voices, but only between the bass and an inner voice. Various dissembling devices are regularly employed to distract attention from or obscure or disguise the presence of the fifths. Example 53 (b) shows the fifth between alto and bass. Soprano, sounding the third above the bass tone, suspends it into the dominant hoping that its nonharmonic dissonance will divert the listener's attention from the inner voices. Example 53 (c) is an attempt to hide the fifths behind a pattern of accompanimental figuration. Although the fifths are indubitably present there is no point at which perfect fifth resolves to perfect fifth.

By far the most frequently used procedure in the resolution of the German Sixth to the dominant triad is one in which the Italian Sixth is substituted for the German Sixth at the point of resolution. Example 53 (d) is but one of many possible melodic arrangements in which the fifth is prominent during the sounding of the German Sixth, but descends to the third in time to permit the Italian sixth resolution to take place: the inner voice third up to the fifth of the dominant, and the melodic third to the third of the dominant. The parallel fifth question is thus adroitly avoided.

The more intricate the relationship of consecutive chords the more crucial the voice-leading. Remote tonalities can be joined together and unexpected chords connected to each other successfully only if there is some element of melody present. The essential melodic movement in the resolution of the German-Italian Sixth described above is only one indication of how the flow of melody is utilized to facilitate theoretically impractical and ungraceful progressions.

XIV

The French Sixth

HENRI WIENIAWSKI (1835-1880) chose to begin the finale of his D Minor Concerto, much favored among violinists, with the third member of the international triumverate of the augmented sixth chords.

EXAMPLE 54. Wieniawski: Violin Concerto, Op. 22, Finale

The French Sixth has, like the Italian and German Sixths, a bass tone which is a half step above the dominant (the diatonic sixth scale step in minor, the chromatically lowered VI in major), the leading tone to the dominant located an augmented sixth above the bass tone, and the tonic of the key acting as the major third of the chord. The fourth tone, which identifies the chord, is the second degree of the prevailing—or soon to prevail—scale. The French Sixth thus includes two augmented intervals: the augmented sixth and the augmented fourth above its bass tone. This combination of intervals is a benefit to students of harmony, for it is easy to recognize when sounded and may be easily and effectively resolved to either the I^6_4 or the V triad.

In Example 54 the augmented sixth is resolved to the doubled dominant tone as in the resolution of the two previously described augmented sixth chords. The augmented fourth (E) is retained as a common tone and becomes the fifth of the dominant chord. The third (D) resolves down by step to the third of the dominant.

An excerpt from a song by a prolific writer of songs shows the alternative resolution.

EXAMPLE 55. H. Wolf: *Tramping*

Example 55 begins at the twenty-first measure of Hugo Wolf's setting of a poem by Edward Mörike. The march-like rhythmic pattern is an indication of the composer's gift for tone-painting, but the harmonic progression is common to many nineteenth-century styles and situations. The song is in D Major and our quotation begins with the IV chord. It is followed by the I^6 but subsequent events make it clear that this I^6 is a pivot chord and from measure two to the cadence the passage is in the key of A. The harmony proceeds from this I^6 of D-IV^6 of A through the I^6_4, V^7 of VI, to VI. The use of the I^6_4 is rather unusual. The usual progression is I^6_4, V^7, VI. The V^7 of VI is substituted for the V^7 of I. It is interesting, though perhaps only coincidental, to note that the vocal melody can be harmonized either way.

The French Sixth appears on the fourth beat of measure four and resolves to the cadential I^6_4. The augmented sixth resolves as usual; the augmented fourth (B) resolves up to the third of the I^6_4; and the third is retained as a common tone.

Example 56 shows the two possible resolutions in the keys of the preceding examples.

EXAMPLE 56

The French, German, and Italian Sixths are basically cadential chords: they announce the dominant so strongly that the tonality is reinforced. Example 54, the beginning of a fully developed large form, hardly appears to be a cadence but it *is*

cadential. The French Sixth unmistakably proclaims the tonality of D, and the composer adds F natural as the upper neighbor to E thereby indicating D minor and not D major. When it resolves to V launching the violin soloist on his appoggiatura-studded arpeggio, the sense of harmonic relaxation is very like a cadential effect. Example 55 is an illustration of the truly cadential French sixth.

The three augmented sixth chords are no more than three variants of a single function: a dramatic method of approaching the dominant triad or the anticipatory (of the dominant triad) tonic triad in second inversion. The Italian Sixth's primary role is the resolution to V, the German Sixth's to resolve to the I_4^6, and the French sixth's to resolve to either. Melodic and textural conditions frequently blur the lines of demarcation between these chords but the interval of the augmented sixth resolving to the doubled dominant is the hallmark of each. Perhaps because of the obscurity of the origin of their names or the obviousness of their common function some theorists are unwilling to admit the importance of their separate analysis. They are presented here as historical realities. They can be nationalistically identified only when their historical functions are understood. When, as later chapters will show, their intervalic construction is committed to other than cadential ends the traditional labels must be dispensed with. If the classical augmented sixth chords are not assimilated as a part of the fundamental vocabulary of chords which provide the basis from which nineteenth- and twentieth-century harmony has grown no facility with contemporary practice is rational.

X V

Augmented Dominants

HARDLY A CHORD, rigidly restricted in its resolution and yet subject to many variations in the details of its connection with other chords, the augmented dominant requires more explanation and discussion than its harmonic influence or frequency of occurrence would seem to warrant.

It is not quite a chord because even more clearly than the chords studied previously it results from contrapuntal motion. If chromatic counterpoint were a more widespread subject of study augmented dominants would not require explanation.

The G sharps and E naturals on the second beat of measure one and the first beat of measure two in Example 57 for instance, are easily recognized as lower neighbors to the F and A naturals which precede and follow them—yet the V-I relationship is unmistakably present. The fifth of the V of IV chord is chromatically raised and thus makes its resolution to the third of the I chord inevitable.

EXAMPLE 57. Moszkowski: *Spanish Dance*

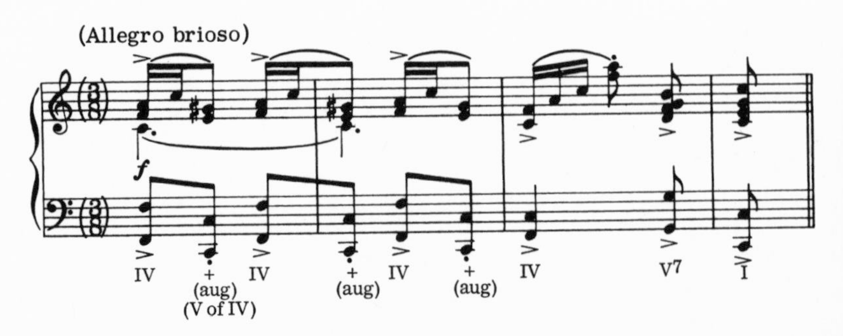

This augmented fifth is the dynamic feature, and its unalterable tendency to resolve upward is so powerful that it may even overcome the tendency of a chord seventh to resolve downward.

Example 58, from the opera *Faust,* illustrates the obvious contrapuntal origin of the chord and the ease with which it resolves to the doubled third of a major triad.

EXAMPLE 58. Gounod: *Faust,* "Waltz"

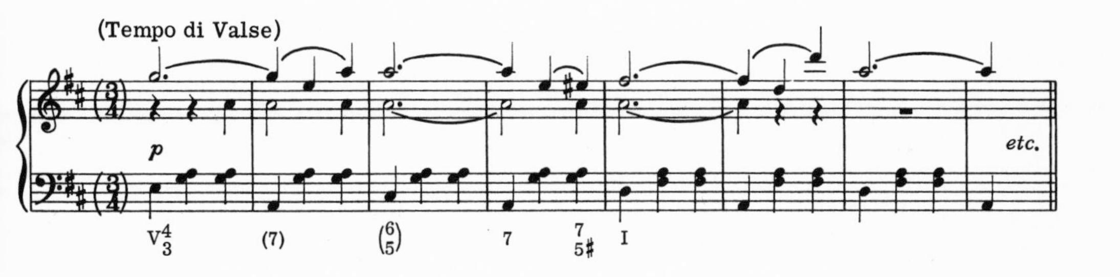

Measure four of the quotation shows the chord fifth augmented to provide a chromatic passing tone to the third of the I chord in measure five. The chord seventh, G, also resolves to the third, and the doubled third, though not usual in major triads, is here perfectly acceptable. The reason is not obscure: the fifth when not augmented normally resolves down by step to the doubled root, and when the fifth is augmented and its resolution thus deflected upward the other voices resolve as usual in dominant seventh to tonic connections.

The simplicity of Example 58 is not always seen in occurrences of chords with augmented fifths however; and Example 59 is a distillation of the various procedures composers have adopted in their use of this chord. It must be remembered that pianistic and orchestral textures, and melodic and contrapuntal circumstances often obscure the straightforward choral appearance of these illustrations: the sound of these tones resolving will emerge from any environment.

EXAMPLE 59

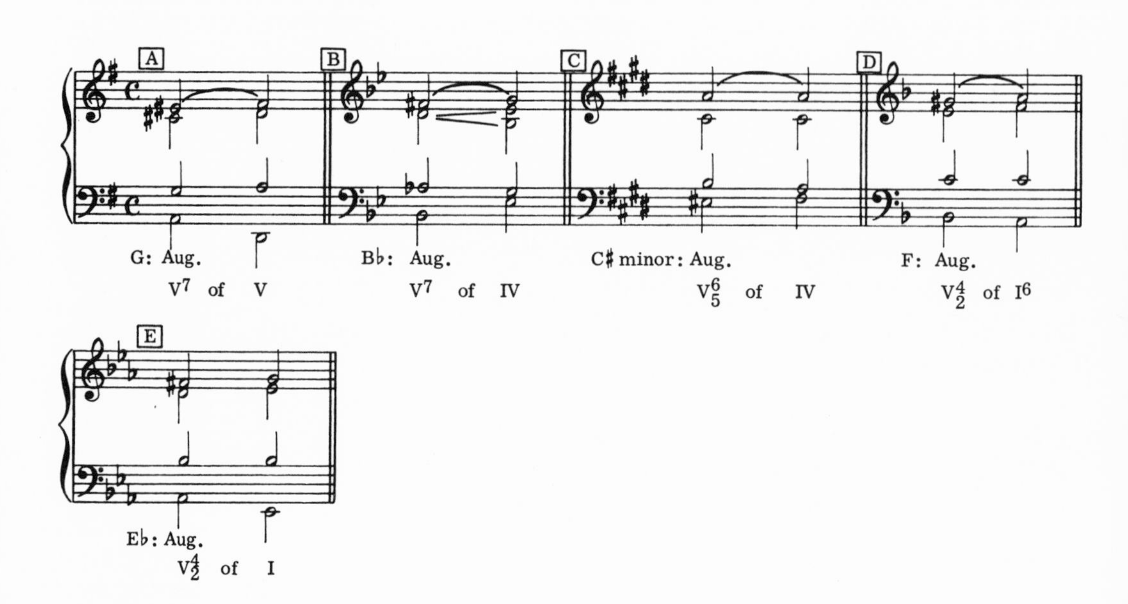

The first thing to be noticed is the root progression: augmented triads and seventh chords always resolve down a perfect fifth or up a perfect fourth as dominants, and usually to major triads. The second conspicuously constant factor is the resolution of the chord third: it always resolves up by step as a leading tone should. Last, and so obvious that it is easily overlooked, is the relative position of the chord tones. The augmented fifth *always* appears above the seventh of the chord. This rule is broken only in highly contrapuntal, complicated, and unusual circumstances.

The management of the chord seventh is not so standardized and Example 59 shows the variations in its resolution.

In Example 59, the seventh resolves upward. The urgency of the augmented fifth is great enough to minimize the dissonance of the seventh, and the perfectly balanced triad (two roots, one third, one fifth) to which the augmented seventh chord resolves justifies the voice leading.

In Example 59 (b), the augmented fifth resolves up by step, the third may either move up a step as a leading tone or, if in an inner voice, may move down a third. The root moves to the root of the chord of resolution and the seventh resolves down by step as its natural tendency dictates, to the doubled third of the major triad which follows.

The minor sixth as the enharmonically spelled augmented fifth is inevitable when the augmented dominant resolves to a minor triad. This is seen in Example 59 (c) where the augmented dominant is inverted. The third in the bass resolves as it does in the resolution of other V^6_5 chords and the other tones of the chord behave similarly. If the key were C sharp major instead of C sharp minor the fifth of the augmented dominant would be G double sharp instead of A, but since A is a diatonic tone in C sharp minor and is also the tone to which the augmented fifth resolves it would be fatuous and unnecessarily confusing to spell it as a true augmented fifth. The sound is clear to the ear and the notation is clear to the eye. The upward resolution of the seventh is not found when the augmented dominant seventh chord is inverted, probably because the dissonant effect of the combined augmented fifth and the unstable bass tone require that the seventh and root of the chord preserve their integrity as diatonically oriented entities.

The third inversion, Example 59 (d), is simply a rearrangement of the tones of (b) and (c). Each tone moves the least possible distance in its resolution, and each moves according to its natural tendency: leading tone and chromatically raised tone up by step and the chord seventh down by step. The root, as its stable and uncomplicated character here permits, remains as a common tone.

Sevenths are dissonant and should resolve down by step—this is a rule which is as fundamental as the law of gravity. Yet we have, in Example 59 (e), a graphic representation of the fact that the seventh of the dominant seventh chord is also the subdominant of the key. As such, it may resolve down a fourth (never up a fifth) to the root of the triad to which it relates as augmented dominant. The three upper voices move as in the preceding example.

In Example 59 the first two (a and b) are rather widely used; but (c), (d), and (e) are rare.

The chromatic augmented dominant triad in first inversion is seen in measures seven and eight of the next quotation. The root of the augmented dominant is doubled and is retained as a common tone to become the doubled fifth of the triad to which it resolves. The augmented fifth and the bass tone (chord third) resolve up by step to the third and root of the major triad. Resolution to a minor triad does not occur, for the effect of chord progression is unconvincing when only one tone moves. Only the third in the bass would move if the resolution were to a minor triad, and its motion would quite likely be heard as that of a non-harmonic tone.

Example 60 also illustrates the profuse use of non-harmonic tones which is typical of late Romantic music. It is not always easy to distinguish between essential and non-essential tones and chords, but if the basis for classification is sound and function the harmonic structure will be clear.

EXAMPLE 60. MacDowell: Op. 31 No. 5

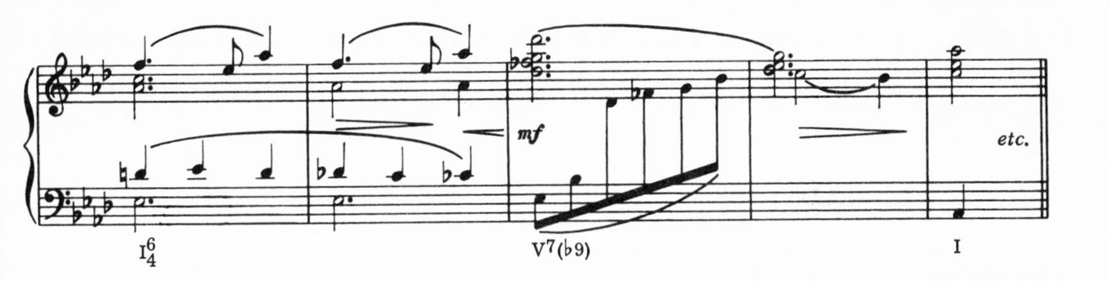

The first three measures of the passage are sounded over the tonic pedal point. The F in measure one appears to be the upper neighbor to E flat, but its occurrence while the E flat below is sustained suggests that it may be the now familiar added major sixth, acceptable because of its consonant sounding membership in the pentatonic scale (A♭, B♭, C, E♭, F in this key). The dominant in measure four, in the second inversion, also includes F, here appearing to be an appogiatura but, perhaps coincidentally, forming the rather rare inverted dominant ninth chord. The chromatic V^7 of VI occurs on the third beat of measure four but its resolution is doubly evaded. Instead of the normal down a fifth resolution the bass moves up by step as in the V^7 to VI resolution (Chapter V). The chord, however, is not the expected root position triad but the triad whose root lies a major second below that of the chromatic dominant. This unusual chord progression is smoothed over by means of non-harmonic devices. The texture is no longer limited to four voices. The quarter note motion in measure five duplicates, in the octave below, the quarter note motion in measure four, thus establishing a contrapuntal relationship between the two measures. These stepwise quarter notes in measure five also serve to blur the harmony a bit, for the G suggests the VII^4_3, the A flat suggests the II^6_5, and the B flat is the root of the II^6.

The V^4_3 which begins measure six becomes, by means of the chromatic quarter notes, a V^6_4 at the end of the measure. The seventh of the dominant is not admissible at this point because its rational resolution would not be possible. If resolved to C the third of the augmented V^6 would be doubled, and the upward resolution, up an augmented second, is equally undesirable. The composer continues the chromatic scale into measure seven, where it becomes the augmented fifth and its resolution.

The chromatic half diminished VII^7 and VII^6_5 of V occur in measures nine and ten as described in Chapter IX. The I^6_4 of measures eleven and twelve is ornamented by chromatic and diatonic non-harmonic tones including the added major sixth as an appoggiatura, and the dominant to which it resolves is the borrowed dominant ninth of the parallel minor key. The effect of the bass E flat remains through measures thirteen and fourteen, and the C, which may be considered as an accented upper neighbor to B flat, a dislocated thirteenth, or an anticipation of the third of the coming tonic triad, maintains the flavor of dissonance which characterizes the whole passage.

The analysis of this passage, in which the inverted augmented dominant is only incidental, was undertaken because it illustrates procedures and practices which require contrapuntal as well as harmonic skills to be understood. Harmonic complexity, with which the remainder of this book is concerned, is essentially a matter of voice leading, and the horizontal lines of music must be as clearly discerned as are the vertical coincidences of melodic pitches called chords. The catalog of labeled chords described in this and the chapters which precede are only points of departure, the grammatical fundament upon which composers have superimposed their own variants, emphases, and colorations. Each previously described harmonic unit must be a familiar member of the musical vocabulary before its influence and elaboration can be understood.

XVI

Augmented Sixth Chords: Variants

FROM THE STOREHOUSE of chords which have won names and definable functions composers have not hesitated to select, adapt and absorb into the fabric of their creativity the harmonic functions, showing only a casual respect for their classical conformation.

Chords of the augmented sixth are conspicuous among the harmonies which have been so adapted. Their functions as described earlier remain in force but their appearance and realization in sound have been adjusted in various ways. The traditional role of these chords is the chromatic approach to the dominant or the tonic six-four chord. Their distinctive feature is the interval of the augmented sixth, and it is the inversion of this interval which is the subject of this chapter.

A baroque chorale melody elaborated and harmonized by J. S. Bach provides an early example of contrapuntal utilization of a harmonic principle.

EXAMPLE 61. J. S. Bach: *The Passion According to St. Matthew*, Recitative, "O Schmerz"

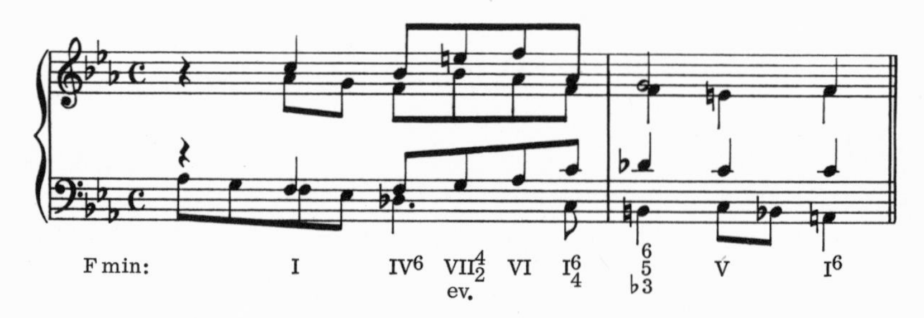

The chord on the first beat of the second measure of Example 61 is obviously composed of a chromatic lower neighbor, a diatonic upper neighbor and a suspension below the diatonic melody. (The minor key signature of one flat less than we now consider correct is common in baroque music.) In function and in pitch membership the chord is a French Sixth, but the augmented sixth is inverted to a diminished third with its lower tone in the bass.

A more widely used adaptation of an augmented sixth chord is shown in Example 62. The piece is in E minor but as our excerpt begins the region of B minor prevails.

EXAMPLE 62. Scriabin: *Prelude*, Op. 11 No. 4

The tonic key is mentioned in measure two and the VII^7 to VI progression is repeated a fourth higher in measures three to four. The D in the melody in measure four is a suspension, and the chord is a major triad on the lowered second scale step in first inversion and with the doubled third—the Neapolitan Sixth of the key. The chord in measure five is similar to the chromaticism of the Bach example, but here the tones are those of the German sixth. Again the augmented sixth is inverted and appears as a diminished third with its lower tone as bass.

In sound, when isolated, this arrangement of pitches is indistinguishable from the dominant $^4_2$ and has been called an enharmonic dominant $^4_2$. It is not wholly dominant in function however, for it preserves the augmented-sixth-chord association with its chord of resolution.

The distant relationship with the prevailing key which upon resolution is found to be not so distant, the chief characteristic of augmented sixth chords, is intensified in this example. It provides a clear example of the strength of tonality, for the I and V chords of an utterly foreign key occur but are not related by the ear to any but the preestablished tonality. The German Sixth and the Neapolitan Sixth bear a dominant to tonic relationship to each other, and if measures four and five are played without reference to preceding and following measures or the tonality of E the chord progression identifies itself as I^6 to V^4_2 of F major. When sounded in context the key of F does not proclaim itself but merges with the tonality of E, demonstrating that tonality need not be disturbed by chromatic coloration, and an established tonal center may include, as here and elsewhere, the twelve tones of the chromatic scale.

Less chromatic in effect than Example 62 the next quotation illustrates chromatic chords approaching tonic and dominant triads: no region of tonality other than C major is suggested before the last two measures.

The tonic C is present as a pedal tone through the first four measures. Measures one and two show an incomplete diminished seventh chord composed of neighbor notes to tones of the tonic triad.

EXAMPLE 63. Tchaikovsky: Op. 39 No. 19

It is of the genre of the chord described in Chapter X, the VII^7 of E minor resolving to VI of E minor, and the fifth, A, is missing because the disposition of essential tones is such that it could not be approached or left except by leap.

In measures three and four the diminished seventh chord of Chapter VIII occurs on the first beats, incomplete because the composer felt that continuation of the pedal tone C to be more desirable than completion of the leading-tone diminished seventh. The second beats of these measures appear to be the borrowed II$^4_2$ chords of the parallel minor key, but the ear hears them as repetitions of the accented beats. The incomplete diminished seventh chord is incomplete because the leading-tone root is missing, a crucial factor in chord analysis. Either definition, II$^4_2$ or incomplete diminished seventh, is theoretically possible, but the leading-tone character of the first beat is too strong to permit the listener to accept the chord on the second beat as a minor subdominant.

Augmented sixth chords make their appearance in measures five and six. The second beats show the true German sixth chord as described in Chapter XIII, but the first beats are duplicates of the pre-I_4^6 chord of Example 62, here resolving to V instead of the I_4^6.

The German Sixth chord is not resolved to V or I_4^6 as expected, but to another arrangement of its tones in measure seven, repeated in measure eight. In Examples 61 and 62 the augmented sixth was inverted to the diminished third with its lower tones as bass. On the first beats of measures seven and eight, Example 63, the augmented sixth remains intact but its lower tone is not the bass tone. The function of the German Sixth is observed in the stepwise resolution to V, but a reminder of simpler chromatic usage occurs in the next to the highest voice. The upper tone of the augmented sixth, F sharp, the leading tone to the dominant is resolved as in the connection of consecutive dominant seventh chords (Chapter IV); chromatically down to the seventh of the dominant seventh. The same chord, this time with C in bass, is sounded on the second beats of measures seven and eight, and all tones are resolved as in the classical resolution of the German Sixth.

The last two measures of the fragment quoted announce a departure from the C major tonality. The melodic motive of measures one and two is here supported by harmonies which contradict the tonal center. The resolution of V to VI of F major is suggested. The $^4_2$ inversion of V resolves gracefully to the root position of V^7 of VI and the key of C recedes as this doorway to new regions of tonality is opened.

There is much to be learned from this example: The tones of each chromatic chord are resolved according to their natural tendencies, the tension created by each dissonance is resolved, and chords which are classically cadential in function are used in various conditions of completeness and incompleteness, root position and inversion, and for the purpose of harmonic incisiveness and variety within the phrase rather than for chromatic embellishment of the cadential formula.

This chapter is intended to demonstrate that creativity is not bound by theoretical rules but that composers have not hesitated to elaborate on the vocabulary of harmonic structures. The expanded range of tonality within a tonal center, the almost harmonic use of non-harmonic tones, and the frequent evasion, postponement, and general obscuring of classical cadential progressions are responsible for the development of late nineteenth-century harmony: it did not grow from a denial of tonality or the invention of "new" harmonic structures or combinations.

XVII

Altered Chords

IF THE DEFINITION of a chord as "the simultaneous sound of three or more different pitches" is accepted no further discussion is necessary; any combination of tones may occur in any context without question. If, on the other hand, it is felt that a chord must be defined as "three or more tones sounding simultaneously to perform a recognizable function within a recognizable tonality" the grammar of the harmonic aspect of musical composition begins to be understood.

Neither of these definitions takes cognizance of the fact that music is, among other things, *sound* in *time,* and that harmony is the result of concurrently sounding melodies. The vocabulary of identifiable harmonic sonorities has been described in Chapters II through XV and each chord has been seen to possess elements which imply resolution. This chapter is concerned with the alteration of one or more elements of familiar chords.

There are two possible reasons for changing the quality of an interval within a chord: to intensify or dramatize its tendency toward resolution or to contradict this natural tendency. The first of these procedures is already familiar. The alteration of diatonic qualities by borrowings from the opposite mode (Chapters VI and VIII); the Neapolitan Sixth chord (Chapter VII), which may be considered an altered II^6; and the augmented dominant (Chapter XV) are obvious examples. Less frequent and less dynamic are alterations which result from contrapuntal motion. The most frequently seen alteration is the chromatic lowering of the fifth of dominant seventh quality chords as seen in Example 64.

EXAMPLE 64. Bruckner, Symphony No. 7, Adagio

The quotation begins on the third beat of the fourth measure of the slow movement of Bruckner's Seventh Symphony. The key of the piece is C sharp minor and the first chord shown is I of that key, but it functions as the pivot chord in a modulation to the region of E major. Consecutive chromatic dominant seventh chords occur, and the V$^4_3$ of VI appears with its fifth lowered on the second beat of its duration. D natural is simply a chromatic passing tone between D sharp and C sharp but it emphasizes the inevitability of the resolution.

The V⁷ of II resolves to II and the key of F sharp minor emerges as D major and A major triads follow and in turn lead to the half cadence.

This example is typical. The dominant seventh chord is the only harmonic unit which can be so drastically altered (a second tritone is added in these examples, creating the sound of the French sixth) without altering its character so completely that it is transformed into a different chord. It is obviously only the fifth which can be chromatically inflected, for neither tthe chromatic lowering or raising of the fifth of the dominant changes its function except to require the most ordinary resolution: down a perfect fifth or up a perfect fourth. Many other chromatic tones may occur in dominants and elsewhere, but will prove to be either non-harmonic or additions such as described in Chapter XXII.

Example 65 includes identically altered dominants, but also demonstrates that such complexities are not always capable of but one analytical explanation.

Example 65. Debussy, *Mazurka*

Measures one and two may be explained in three different ways. One identifies the progression as a series of dominant sevenths resolving in the circle of fifths: G sharp, C sharp, F sharp, B. The dominant on G sharp is altered, its fifth in the bass is lowered; and the A in the upper voice is a neighboring tone. The dominant on F sharp is altered in the same way and is further complicated by the fact that the suspended G sharp does not resolve down to the root (F sharp) until the chord has changed to B. Such delayed resolutions of non-harmonic tones are by no means rare.

A second defensible analysis invokes the concept of parallelism,* justified by the fact that the three lower voices are parallel descending chromatic scales. The root progression is thus D, C♯, C♮, B. The first G sharp in measure one is non-harmonic, A being the chord tone, and the seventh is spelled enharmonically (B sharp instead of C natural) because of the time honored practice of spelling the half step below the dominant as a raised fourth (see the discussion of this point in connection with Example 16 in Chapter IV). This principle is not violated by the C natural on the first beat of measure two, for chord roots are invariably spelled according to their function. The A sharp instead of B flat as the seventh above C may also be attributed to the common practice of chromatic scale spelling. In minor keys the lowered fourth is replaced by the raised third. The suspended G sharp is the augmented fifth and eventually resolves to A as required.

A less convincing but plausible view holds that measure one is the French Sixth to V^7 progression of F sharp minor, and measure two is the same progression in E major—a stepwise harmonic sequence. The A in measure one and the suspended G sharp in measure two are non-harmonic as in the circle of fifths concept.

The final two measures offer no such opportunity for contrasting views: the subdominant bass tone on the first beat, the II^6_5 on the second, and the V^7 on the third beat resolving to the ornamented I chord in the next measure are conventionally cadential.

The second reason for chord alteration—the contradiction of the basic tendency to resolve—may be observed here. The final chromatic dominant seventh chord of the series is rooted

* See Chap. XVIII.

on B; and B is the subdominant tone of the prevailing key. The dominant quality is canceled, and without change of root the harmony becomes subdominant in function, the II^6_5.

It is interesting to experiment with alteration and other harmonic novelties, but such investigation will be fruitless unless it grows out of the absolute mastery of the vocabulary and grammar of tonal harmony. Study of the works of the masters of this art will show how cautiously, though effectively, innovations are attempted.

XVIII

Parallelism

SERIES OF CHORDS of the same or similar quality in stepwise root progression are not rare. They occur in diatonic harmony usually as consecutive first inversions of triads, such as the progression I^6, II^6, III^6, IV^6, V^6, VI^6, VII^6, I^6. Parallel chromatic chords serve a greater variety of purposes and involve a wider diversity of harmonies.

Our first example shows the simplest form of chromatic parallelism: The harmonization of the chromatic scale.

EXAMPLE 66. Chopin, *Polonaise*, Op. 53

Example 66 is the opening of Chopin's famous A♭ *Polonaise* announcing a motive which occurs, with various minor modifications, four times during the sixteen measures of introduction to the principal theme. The *sforzando* four octave E flat is a consistent feature. It acts as a dominant pedal point and does not resolve to the tonic A flat until the seventeenth measure.

The upward chromatic sweep to the first beat of measure two reflects a device which is extremely common in music of the seventeenth century: a simple melodic fragment of the chromatic scale used to embellish, color, vary, or emphasize a melodic line or a single important tone. Essentially non-harmonic in character, this touch of coloratura was a special favorite of Mozart, who in Chopin's view could do no wrong.

The noteworthy aspect of Chopin's use of the device is his use of parallel major triads in first inversion to harmonize the ascending chromatic half steps, and each triad is notated in its most recognizably familiar form. A major, B major and C sharp major are far removed from the A flat major landscape: B double flat, C flat, and D flat are certainly more closely related to the key of the piece, but the composer wisely chose the notation which is most legible to the performer—chord successions which have a diatonic existence—V^6 to VI^6 progressions from the keys of D minor, E minor, F sharp minor and G minor. The notation of harmonies which move in unaccustomed ways is often problematic, and Chopin's method is easily the most practical and is widely used whenever possible.

Before proceeding to the analysis of the next example, only the inverted augmented sixth chord on the third beat of measure two need be mentioned. Its position in the key, intervallic structure and resolution are identical to the first augmented sixth chord of Example 63 (p. 106). It here serves to reinforce the dominant as the tension of the unresolved introductory pedal point is maintained, while in Example 63 it is simply one of many chromatic approaches to the V chord within the formal phrase-structure.

The parallel chords of Example 67 cannot be spelled according to a diatonic relationship because no diatonic key center includes dominant seventh chords a half step apart. The role of this excerpt in the composition in which it occurs is also different from the purpose of Chopin's harmonized chromatic scale. Grieg's *Nocturne,* in C major, includes various harmonic patterns, among them progressions which feature descending chromatic bass lines, both harmonic and non-harmonic.

EXAMPLE 67. Grieg: *Nocturne,* Op. 54 No. 4

Example 67 demonstrates a second function of chromatic parallelism. It occurs as the end of the second statement of the limpid and nocturnal principal theme, when the form has been rounded off and the idea of the composition completely realized. Its function is to summarize and intensify the chromatic spectrum of harmonic colors of the preceding sections of the work while dissolving its melodic motive in an indeterminate and unstable series of flats and sharps. The dominant seventh chord qualities are here simply appropriate vehicles for the effect: in other situations or other eras any chord quality or interval combination could be used to create the same effect of dissolution of tonal progression and contraction of phrasing and harmonic rhythm.

Grieg's sense of tonality led him to bring the progression to a halt on the dominant, and it is not easy to find a similar passage which does not lead to a pause on a tonal degree of a preestablished tonality. Dissolution of harmony and fragmentation of melody have rarely completed the summing up of a musical idea, and as in Grieg's *Nocturne* in which a codetta referring to previous events follows these parallel dominants, most composers who have used this device have done so to prepare the listener for the broadened time-scale of the final cadence. Such harmonic retardation is so constant a factor in the closing phrases of musical works that it is a source of amazement to hear a performance which includes elaborate retardations of tempo to imply the ends of movements.

A third instance of parallelism is illustrated in Example 68. Here the final cadence has been reached, the formal presentation of all thematic, developmental, and pictorial events has been completed, and nothing remains to be done except the final statement of ending.

Example 68. Berlioz, Symphony Fantastic, First movement

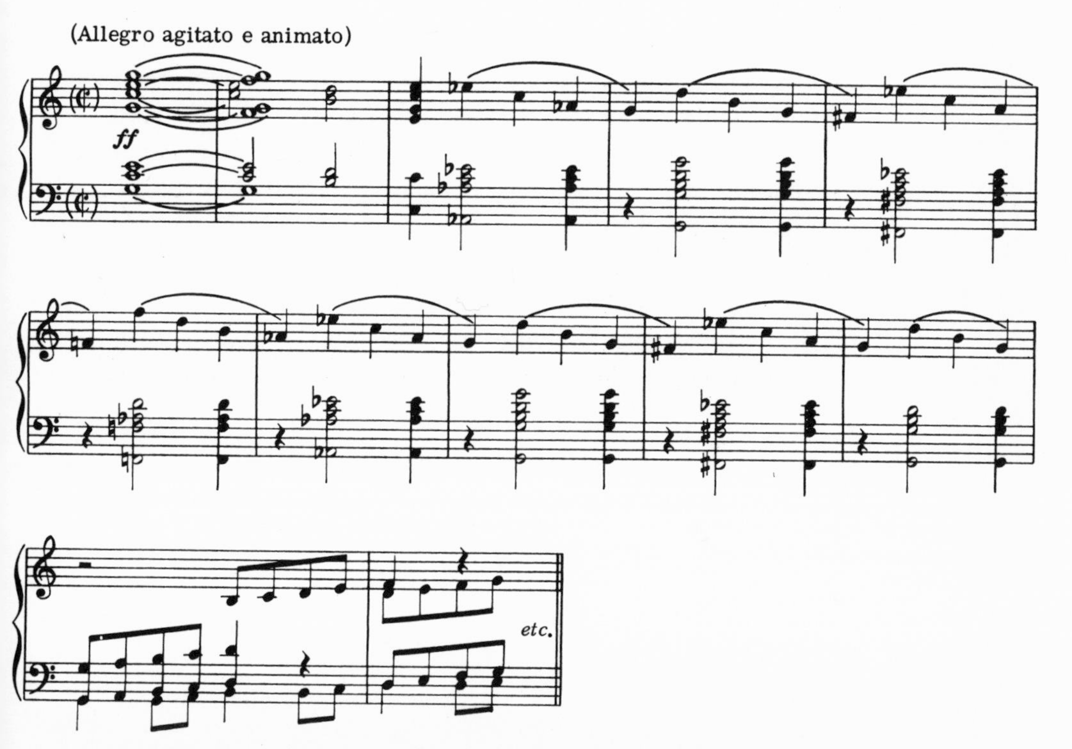

Berlioz, after the romantically impassioned portrayals of the opening movement of his symphony have been worked out, arrives at the powerful I_4^6, V^7, I cadence which begins our quotation. The passage which follows (to measure ten) consists of four measures of major triads and diminished seventh chords arranged in parallel motion over a chromatically descending bass line. The last diminished seventh chord is resolved as described in Chapter VIII, ending the parallelism as it resolves to the dominant whose semicadential effect serves as a steppingstone to the following episode (measure eleven) of the coda.

This aspect of the principle of parallelism is one which is subject to a wide variety of applications. It takes no part in significant melodic, contrapuntal, or harmonic developments but is a valuable means of preserving or even creating an atmosphere of uncertainty and instability. It is also valuable as a means of preserving rhythmic motion and textural continuity while truly pertinent developmental operations are suspended: a most useful device for composers of large scale works in which pace and proportion are important factors, and one which evidence proves to be not unknown in the smaller forms of composition.

The basic technics of parallelism are simple: all harmonic voices move in the same direction, no real tonal center is established or implied, and no change of texture is invoked while the parallel passage is in progress. The parallel harmonies are usually fitted to a chromatically descending bass line but intermingled major and minor second relationships are not rare and even wider intervals have been known to occur between roots. The chord qualities may or may not be consistent but the parallel passage will consist of triads, seventh chords or other formations exclusively; not a mixture of harmonic personalities.

Other manifestations of parallelism are visible in more recent musical expressions. Melodic lines doubled at the fifth, fourth, or other interval instead of the traditional octave or third, and parallel harmonic motion in combination with a tonal or other contrasting texture in another register are resources which have become rather commonplace since the turn of the century.

To the student of nineteenth-century harmony, parallelism must be what Martian climatology is to the twentieth-century student of science: fascinating and apparently vital. Opportunities for first-hand research are rare however, and a vast amount of earthbound study must precede any practical application of the general principles described in this chapter. Recognition of parallelism and the ability to analyze its component parts and its function in context are all that is asked: our subject of study is chord progression, not arrested harmonic motion.

XIX

Mediant Relationships

THE RELATIONSHIP of VI and III to I of the major mode was widely utilized by nineteenth-century composers. These mediant scale degrees (halfway between the tonic and dominant in the ascending scale, halfway between the tonic and subdominant in the descending scale) offer opportunities for chromaticism beyond that of altered diatonic chords, chords borrowed from closely related keys, and the specialized group of traditionally cadential augmented sixth and Neapolitan chords. Roots moving in fourths and fifths are strongly predominant in the works of Classical composers. Romantic and post-Romantic writers made use of other relationships as well, and the connection of mediants —chords a third apart—is conspicuous among them.

In Example 69 Ludwig van Beethoven points out how agreeably the tonic and lower major mediant can be associated.

EXAMPLE 69. Beethoven, *Bagatelle,* Op. 33 No. 1

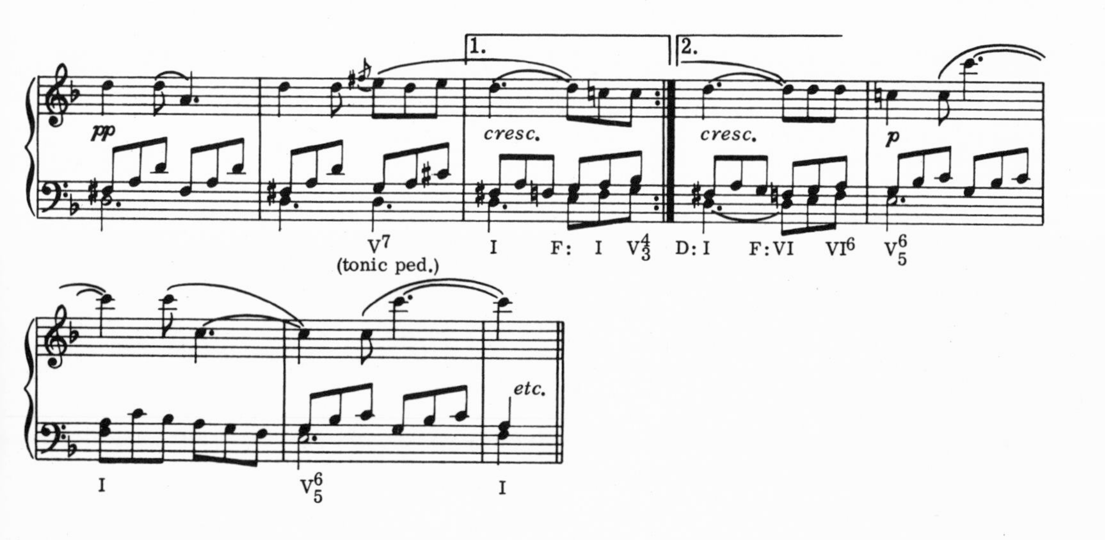

The harmony of the first four measures is simply the tonic and dominant seventh chords of F major: the second phrase, without even a hint of modulation to establish a new key, is wholly in D major. The original key is unaffectedly restored in the first and second endings and in the following section, only the beginning of which is shown, proceeds in the undimmed tonality of F.

Beethoven's little *Bagatelle* shows the ease with which a mediant key is accepted as a region or color within the tonic environment. Example 70 shows an isolated mediant chord.

EXAMPLE 70. Liszt: *Sonetto 47 del Petrarca*

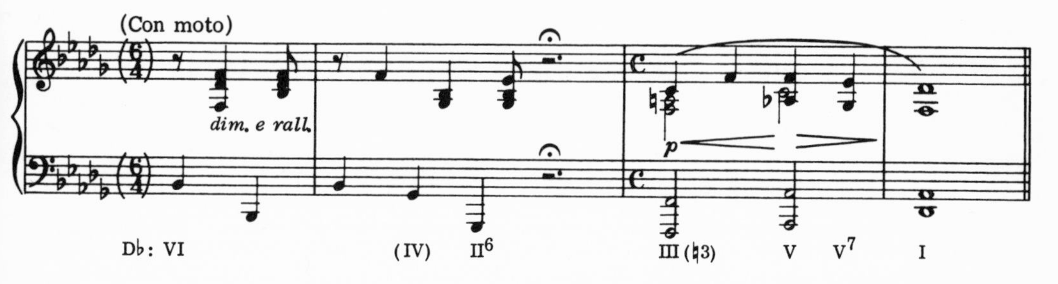

The chord on the first beat of the common-time measure is the major triad of the upper mediant and appears without preparation of any sort. There are other explanations for this occurrence, and the importance of the identification of this triad as a mediant is minimal. The chords which precede it, the VI, IV, II^6 of D flat, may also be described (and are heard) as the I, VI, IV^6 of B flat minor, in which case the F major triad is the diatonic dominant triad and the change to D flat takes place as the major third of the F major triad becomes A flat, the third of the III chord of D flat.

A second possible analysis presents itself if pre-Classical modal harmony is considered. The Phrygian mode, when there are five flats in the key signature, begins and ends on F and its tonic chord is major in quality. This progression of II^6 to major upper mediant appears to be a typical Phrygian cadential progression. Inasmuch as many nineteenth and twentieth-century composers use modal melodies and harmonies in their works it is well to be aware of the possibility of such reflections of a musical language which was not oriented to the major-minor system, and to be equipped to recognize them.

It is quite conceivable that the composer simply changed the quality of the III chord in order to inject a bright chromatic color at the cadence. This third possible analysis is easy to defend, for diatonic roots are frequently seen to support chords which contain chromatic tones. The major III of the present quotation and the minor IV and half-diminished II^7 in major are examples. It is safer, however, to seek a less arbitrary explanation than simply to classify all such instances as "change of quality," for it is important that the source, purpose, and character of the change be clearly understood.

The ease of connection of the tonic triad to the mediants is illustrated in the abstract in Example 71. Points to be noted are that stepwise motion predominates, that there are no cross-relations, the major third relationship may be notated as a diminished fourth, and the minor third relationship as an augmented second.

EXAMPLE 71

A more complex and typically Wagnerian harmonic progression is our next subject for discussion. Non-harmonic tones abound, no cadential point of relaxation is arrived at and the whole fabric of this forward driving texture results from the skillful mixture of chromatic harmony with clearly harmonically inspired melodic elements.

EXAMPLE 72. Wagner, *Die Meistersinger*, Act II

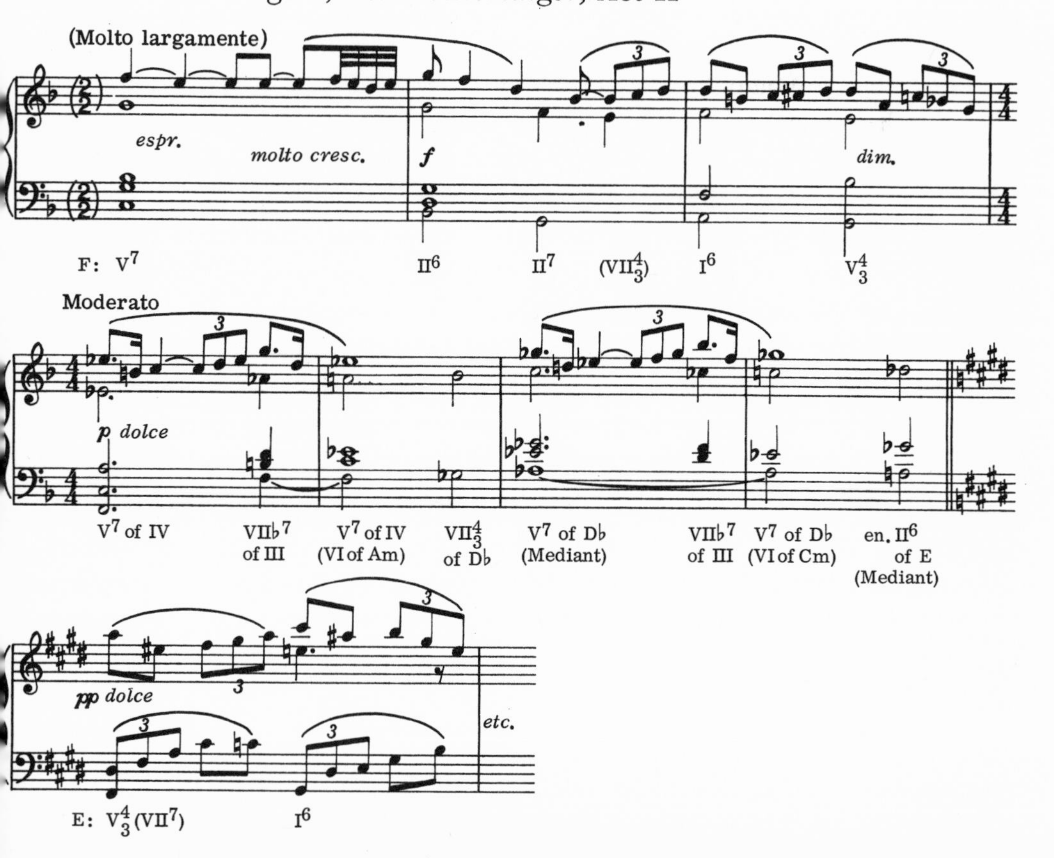

The quotation begins in F major. In measure four the minor seventh is added to the tonic triad, changing its function to that of V^7 of IV. This dominant seventh quality prevails through measures four and five: the common tone (evaded resolution, Chapter X) diminished seventh chord, enharmonically spelled, on the third quarter of measure four has a purely neighboring tone non-harmonic effect and the VII^4_3 of D flat in the second half of measure five consists of passing tones in sound. This inverted leading tone seventh chord is a good example of contrapuntal harmony. Though definitely "passing tone" in effect, it coincidentally prepares the way for the coming region of tonality.

Measures six and seven are almost duplicates of measures four and five in the key of the lowered upper mediant (V^7 of B♭ major to V^7 of D♭ major, the progression of roots from F to A flat); the only alteration being the slight change of quality of the chord on the second half of the second measure (measure seven) of the repeated pattern. This time it forms the II^6 of the coming key, spelled enharmonically because of the D flat environment in which it occurs. The succession of mediants is B flat, D flat, E (not F flat for reasons of ease of notation and legibility), and the composer has accomplished a modulation from F up (not down) to E.

If longer quotations were possible it could be shown that as the eighteenth century waned and the nineteenth century waxed and waxed more strongly, mediant relationships were more and more widely exploited. Where Classical composers depended upon the tonic-dominant relationship for contrast between different sections of their compositions, later writers frequently utilized mediant keys for secondary themes and other non-tonic episodes.

Major keys on the diatonic third and sixth degrees and on the chromatically lowered third and sixth degrees are the most frequently encountered keys. Never definable, theoretically or aurally, as relative minor or major associates of the principal key, the mediant relationship has assumed a significance easily equal to that of the less usual diatonic relationships such as I major and V minor, III minor, and II and VII minor and major.

The profuseness of accidentals involved in the connection of tonic and mediant chords and keys should not be permitted to obscure the essentially close affinity which exists so clearly when heard rather than seen. The sound of the music represented by the fragmentary glimpses given in the examples in this chapter is all that is required to demonstrate that knowledge of the manner of its notation must be gained by all who aspire or claim to be musicians.

X X

Tritone Root Relationships

DIABOLUS IN MUSICA, the devil in music, according to musicians of a pretonal era, was the tritone—the troublesome interval of the diminished fifth or augmented fourth. Modern students understand the feeling which engendered the label but undoubtedly there is a difference between the particulars which prompted the antique nomenclature and the contemporary student apprehension.

Chromatically minded composers, however, do not hesitate to utilize the facts that the tone a diminished fifth below or an augmented fourth above the tonic is the leading tone to the dominant, and the diatonic progression VI to II in minor is a tritone. Once established as an acceptable member of the community on this basis it was not difficult to promote the interval to the responsible position of successive chord roots in chromatic progressions. An important step in this promotion was the advent of the Neapolitan Sixth (Chapter VII). Its inversion is due to the undeniably felt need for a diatonic bass tone but the interval of root connection is a tritone. This first step is an almost diatonic progression in Example 73.

EXAMPLE 73. Franck, *Finale*, Op. 21

The chord progression is simple: I, VI (could this be the source of the Neapolitan relationship?) V^7 of V to V. The melodic lines dictate the voice leading; the chord tones are fitted in beneath the melody where the organist can reach them with his right hand while his left hand plays the quarter note pattern of outlined chords. The bass is played on the pedal keyboard.

Another justification for tritone connections is the fact that dominant seventh chords whose roots are a diminished fifth or an augmented fourth apart have their thirds and sevenths in common as shown in Example 74:

EXAMPLE 74

The enharmonic common tones may be spelled according to the chord of resolution thus the first chord may be spelled C, E, A♯, appearing to be a chord of the augmented sixth and suggesting a relationship with the key of E and the progression German, French, or Italian Sixth, V^7 of V, I^6_4, V^7 I. The ease with which these two seemingly remote dominants can be intermingled is seen in Example 75.

EXAMPLE 75. Brahms, *Capriccio,* Op. 76 No. 8

Measure one of Example 75 is here used to ornament the dominant seventh of C major. The arpeggiated D flat triad in the bass clef combined with the third and seventh of the dominant of C above forms an enharmonically spelled chromatic dominant $^4_3$. Its bass tone is the lowered sixth step of the scale, the upper neighbor to the dominant and often used bass tone (see Chapters XII, XIII, XIV, and XVI) for cadential embellishment. An unusual touch is the concurrent sounding of D flat and C sharp. C sharp is the lower neighbor of the D natural to which it resolves in the second measure and D flat is the root of the D flat triad.

A more straightforward example of harmonic progression is seen in the following Example 76:

EXAMPLE 76. Dvorak, Symphony No. 5, Largo

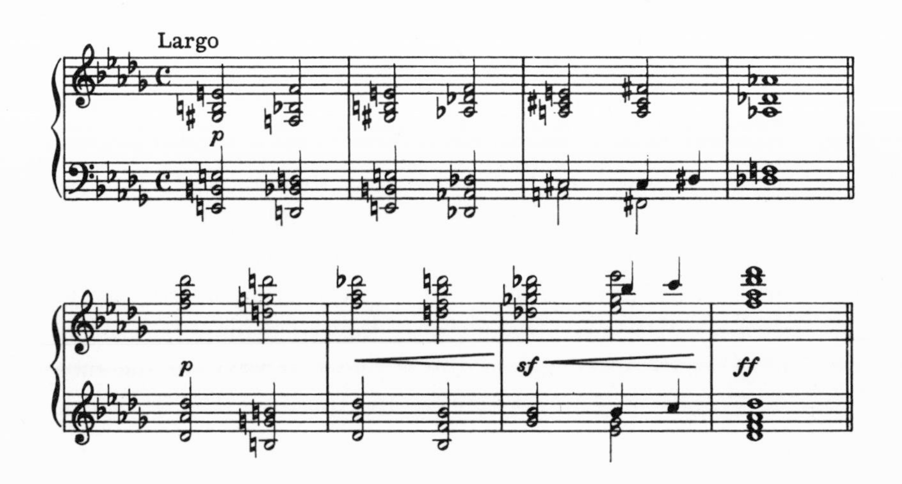

For the beginning of the second movement of his *New World Symphony* Dvorak chose to use a harmonic modulation from the key of the first movement (E) to the key of the second (D flat). This unusual practice provides us with a striking illustration of non-dominant chromatic chord progression.

The tonic effect of E is immediately shattered by the B flat chord, the triad whose root is at the opposite pole of the circle of keys, the tritone relationship. There are no dominant implications in these chords and the fluency of association described above is wholly absent. The return to E on the first beat of measure two is followed by a succession of mediants, E, D flat (enharmonic C sharp), A, F sharp, which successfully dispel any remaining vestige of tonality. The final chord of the series, the F♯ minor triad, functions as the minor IV (enharmonic) of D flat and, with the quarter note passing tone helping to emphasize the resolution, triumphantly settles on D flat in a plagal cadence. This is a unique example, for it almost appears to be a result of theoretical intellectualism: how to modulate convincingly from a major key to the major key a minor third below, using only seven chords, all triads and without any suggestion of a dominant function or association between them.

The second four measures of Example 76 occur at a later stage of the movement and though identical in texture and style, and immediately recognizable as a recurrence of the opening phrase, are not as complex as the passage they imitate. The tritone progression—D flat, G, D flat—and the mediant progression of major triads down a minor and then a major third are repeated. Measure three continues the mediant progression but is diatonic in effect: IV, II, VII^6 to I in measure four. No modulation is called for at this point in the movement and the passage here serves as a reinforcement of the D flat tonality, aided by the I, I, IV, I progression on the strong first beats of the measures.

Tritone chord connections are thus seen to be versatile in effect and usefulness. Example 16, Chapter IV, should be reexamined in connection with the examples of this chapter. Although once considered only devilish, it is now realized that the tritone may be turned to useful ends in establishing, ornamenting, reinforcing, contradicting, or obliterating tonality.

XXI

Stepwise Root Relationships

STEPWISE ROOT PROGRESSIONS are the least frequent of all chord connections in tonal situations. Parallelism (Chapter XVIII) and the diatonic and chromatic equivalents of IV to V, V to VI, and III to IV account for the vast majority of instances of its use, and even these are outnumbered by the movement of roots in fifths, fourths, and thirds. Stepwise resolutions involving chromaticism and not definable as one of the above are even more rare and are the subject of this chapter.

Major triads that are separated by seconds, and not V to VI (minor) or IV to V (major), are the first to be considered. Such progressions, probably because of their disassociation with dominant and subdominant tendencies, invariably suggest a pretonal atmosphere. The Dorian mode includes major triads on III and IV, the Phrygian on II and III, and the Aeolian on VI and VII. Many composers of the present and the not too distant past have made good use of these modal harmonic colors. Their Classical and early Romantic predecessors rarely ventured more than an occasional modal melody superimposed over major or minor harmony.

It is quite possible to explain the progression of chords as exclusively tonal in the following:

EXAMPLE 77. Faure, *Requiem,* Introit

Measures one through eight are diatonic chords of the natural minor scale of D: I, V, III, VI, III indicating the tonal center of F major in the last two or three measures. The E flat major triads in measure nine, ten, and thirteen require that the key of B flat major be admitted, for in our tonal system E flat and F major triads can occur only in that key. In measures thirteen to fourteen, where the chord roots are E flat, F, G flat, the effect of parallelism is not convincingly heard, and we must consider that B flat minor has been tapped—the G flat chord is VI of that key and a practice described in Chapter VI has been invoked. The G flat chord is in second inversion and resolves to the V^7 of G flat, a succession of sounds which exists only in the key of G flat major. The V^7 of G flat is, if its seventh is thought of as B natural instead of C flat, the German sixth of the previously heard key of F and resolves to the I^6_4 of that key. Its appearance here as a chromatic dominant is not an oddity, for composers are usually more concerned with simple clarity of notation than with theoretical explanations. A familiar and easily recognizable progression is I^6_4 V^7 and Fauré saw no reason to write it in any other way.

The resolution of this chromatic dominant—enharmonic German sixth is also irregular, for the C flat–B natural resolves to A (note the precedent in the diminished third of the resolution of the Neapolitan sixth), the doubled third, instead of to C. The implication of this reinforced A is borne out as the resolution of the I^6_4 of F is evaded and the tonality is again deflected. The final cadence is on A, and the cadential progression is plagal. The subdominant role in the plagal cadence is here played by the II^6_5 of the parallel minor, a rather frequently seen modification of the classical formula.

Every chord in this quotation is tonal, tonic, dominant, or subdominant, yet their treatment does not suggest a diatonic equivalent. The tonal centers observed are D, F, B flat, G flat, and A, and in spite of the consistently solemn and deliberate tone of the piece it is a clear example of expanded tonality.

If modal influences are sought a simpler analysis is possible. Measures one to eight are made entirely of tones of the Aeolian mode on D, and its descending scale provides the bass line. In measures nine to thirteen where the tone E flat contradicts the preceding mode, the Aeolian mode on G, the subdominant may be assumed. Measure fourteen does not fit into any reasonable modal conception but is a clearly nineteenth-century interjection. Measures fourteen to sixteen establish the dominant, the Aeolian mode on A. The major quality of the final triad is *de rigeur* in modal music.

The cadence in the dominant key is typical of sectional compositions such as this *Requiem,* for the key opening of subsequent sections is thus prepared.

Example 77 is a simplified version of the original. Fauré's *Requiem* is scored for chorus, orchestra, and organ and does not fit gracefully on two staves. All parts are shown in the example but octave doublings are omitted.

Connections of chord roots a major second apart, when a tonal definition is unjustifiable, are usually explainable as modal. Half step connections require further discussion.

EXAMPLE 78. Schumann, *Papillons,* Op. 2

Measures three and four of Example 78 show a departure from the key which appears to be drastically remote; but when viewed in context are seen to be simply a half step displacement, a sort of sequence in reverse of the root connection of measures five and six. The E flat dominant $^6_5$ to A flat is followed by the dominant $^6_5$ to A, and the A is V^4_2 of the key.

Such half step (above or below) displacements may not be participants in any harmonic development but simply colors which relate only to the preceding and following chords. There are, however, chromatic half step relationships in tonal music: the Neapolitan triad to the tonic and the augmented sixth chords to the dominant. Many apparently inexplicable harmonic events become clear when it is realized that the expansion of tonality develops through the expansion of chord resolution. The Neapolitan Sixth of C, for example is a D flat major triad. The way is therefore open to the use of roles of the D flat major triad: it may be resolved as the V of G flat, IV of A flat, I of D flat, VI of F minor, or its root may serve as the bass tone of an augmented sixth chord in F major or minor. When it is remembered that any major quality diatonic chord may be resolved as a Neapolitan or other chromatic chord the ever widening range of tones and tonal regions within an undisturbed tonal center will be perceived.

Whole step root connections may be tonal or pretonal in origin, half step connections are among the most sophisticated chromaticisms. Either may occur as an isolated chord or two, in sequence with progressions more clearly related to the prevailing tonality, or, as connections of keys rather than only chords, as regions of tonality in whole sections of large or small compositions.

XXII

Expanded Chords

IT IS PERHAPS only logical to expect that as chordal functions and the interrelationships of keys were broadened in scope the indomitable companions to harmonic progression, non-harmonic tones, would also assume new roles. The subject of this chapter is non-harmonic tones which have become identified with certain chord qualities so specifically that they come very close to being chord tones.

The pentatonic scale is surely the most widely utilized basis for melodic expression and it is frequently superimposed over major triads without implying any contradiction of their function. The final measures of an etude by Frederic Chopin show that the composer felt that after the customary cadence has been completed no minimization of the tonic effect would be felt if the tones of the pentatonic scale, which are not included among the tones of the tonic triad, are sounded in the concluding arpeggio.

EXAMPLE 79. Chopin, *Etude*, No. 26

Harmonically speaking, these tones are the added sixth and ninth above the root. They have been seized upon and flagrantly exploited by practitioners of music whose purposes and accomplishments limit rather than encourage development of the art of music,* but they have also been accepted as consonant members of the tonic triad by musicians whose object is the preservation of tonality in the presence of dissonance. There is enough evidence in our musical heritage to warrant serious consideration of their claim to validity.

Even more obvious is the ornamentation of dominant seventh chords. No chord is more clearly identifiable. The third above the root of a dominant on G establishes the fact that the chord does not belong to a key which requires even one flat in its signature. The seventh announces that there are no sharps present either, and the key of C is inevitably present. This proclamation of the tonal center is clear whenever a root, major third, and minor

* See Appendix, P. 171ff.

seventh are sounded together. There are only two tones which can obscure the dominant function of this combination of tones: the major seventh above the root because it is the leading tone to the already present root; and the perfect fourth above the root because it is the destination tone of the structure and the only reason for its existence. All other tones of the chromatic scale are admissible and will resolve to the indicated tonic chord.

EXAMPLE 80. The chromatic scale (shown over ascending mediant roots) in V7 chords.

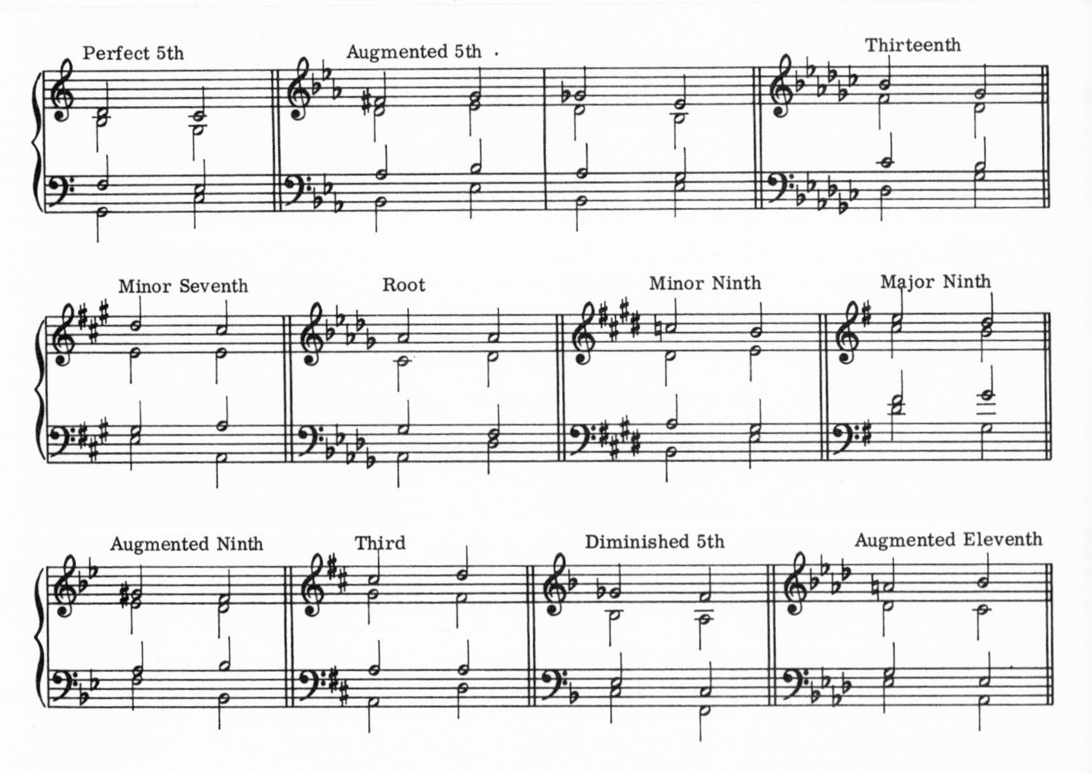

These added tones are usually approached and left by step and may usually be defined as passing tones, appoggiaturas, suspensions, or neighboring tones; but it is difficult to deny their significance in Example 81.

Example 81. Liszt: *Il Penseroso*

Measure one of Example 81 poses a question: is the dominant $\frac{4}{3}$ altered or not? The harmonic function of non-harmonic tones is clearly presented here.

Consecutive dominants and the circle of fifths (Chapter IV) are the basis on which the following measures are constructed. The tonic of C sharp minor is altered to become V^7 of F sharp. It is complete with root, third, fifth, and seventh. The fifth is suspended to become the major ninth of the dominant on F sharp. It is hardly a genuine suspension because it does not resolve to the doubled root of the F sharp chord but is chromatically lowered to become the minor ninth instead. The minor ninth is suspended over the bar line and resolves to the fifth of the dominant on B, but the sound of the suspended tone is quite harmonic in effect and its classification must be somewhere between that of chord tone (enharmonic misresolved augmented fifth), and non-chord tone. The major and minor ninth appear over the dominant on E as in the preceding measure over F sharp.

The chord on the first beat of measure four interrupts the sequence and delays the resolution of the preceding dominant.

Instead of the expected dominant seventh on A a chord appears in which the upper voices follow the sequential pattern of the preceding measure but with the bass tone A sharp instead of A. A half-diminished to diminished sound results. It is non-harmonic in origin, for if a complete dominant on A were to be sounded on the first beat no change of bass tone would occur on the next accent and the established harmonic rhythm would be disrupted. The composer chose to incorporate in the II^6_5 V^7 semicadential measure a chromatic bass line in imitation of the upper voice rather than to permit a static bass.

Measures two, three, and four are then repeated, but with modifications. Minor ninths are added to the dominant on C sharp and B, and an appoggiatura is inserted before the fifth of the dominant on C sharp, thus creating a uniform quality of sound with the chord in the first beats of measure three and six. These minor ninths are undeniably chord tones. It is only the syncopation of the melodic line and the harmonic-suspension effect of the G natural over B which can bring doubt to the belief that the upper voice is equally harmonic throughout.

The thirteenth is also often seen in dominant seventh chords, usually explainable as a non-harmonic tone but often clearly harmonic. (See Chapter IX, Example 31.)

Diminished seventh chords may also include a tone or two in addition to the four which identify it. The diminished seventh quality is obliterated by any tone which is not a major ninth above one of the four tones of the basic chord as described in Chapter X, Examples 38 and 39. Five tone diminished seventh chords appear in Example 72 in Chapter XVIII and are repeated here:

EXAMPLE 82. Wagner: *Die Meistersinger,* Act III

The G in the first and B flat in the second diminished chord are approached and left by leap and permit no convincing non-harmonic definition. That the composer felt them to be harmonic is demonstrated by the spelling. In the first diminished seventh the A flat to A natural would logically and normally be spelled G sharp to A, the leading tone to tonic relationship. But because of the presence of G natural as an essential tone, G sharp is inadmissible as another essential tone, and the chord is spelled as if the root were G—which it is not. The same conditions prevail in the second diminished chord where the enharmonic tone is C flat instead of B natural.

The spacing between chord tones in all expanded chords is extremely important: their functions and tonality are obscured if their spatial relationships are not observed. In general it may be assumed that the following rules apply:

1. The interval of a second does not occur except between the root and seventh of the chord, for a non-harmonic tone may be implied when essential chord tones are intended.
2. Ninths appear at least a ninth, elevenths at least an eleventh, and thirteenths at least a thirteenth above the chord root. The concept of chords in thirds is preserved: third, fifth, seventh, ninth, eleventh, and thirteenth retain their intervallic relationship to the root of the harmonic structure.

Non-harmonic tones become increasingly frequent and wield a more significant effect on the harmony which they supposedly ornament as the nineteenth century merges into the twentieth. Many a "modern" sounding composition is so only because it utilizes formerly purely melodic embellishing tones as essential chord tones. This chapter has only scratched the surface of this aspect of harmony: only extensive analysis of the literature of the period will show its influence.

XXIII

Harmonic Sequence

THE WEALTH of color and diversity of tonal relationships which are so prominently flaunted in the study of chromatic harmony have prompted many extended sequential passages which avoid tedium and obvious repetitiousness where similarly designed diatonic sequences would surely flag. Consecutive dominants and progressions through mediant keys have already been illustrated and sequential progressions can be seen in the chapters on those subjects and in almost any sizable chromatic composition encountered in general musical experience.

Effective passages can be made of the simplest material. Every student knows, it is hoped after Chapter XV, that augmented triads inevitably imply resolution to the major triad whose root is a perfect fourth above or a perfect fifth below—the dominant to tonic relationship. Giacomo Puccini used this simple principle in the composition of one of the most telling of his operatic scenes.

EXAMPLE 83. Puccini, *Madame Butterfly,* Act I

The harmonic pattern is major triad, augmented triad a minor third below, major triad. This formula rises from the A flat triad in measure one through B flat, C, and D major chords. The D major triad is inverted in the second half of measure seven and followed by an augmented quality dominant functioning seventh chord. It resolves to E, continuing the upward sequence, and may be considered the French Sixth of A resolving to V or the altered (lowered fifth) dominant $\frac{4}{3}$ of E resolving to I. Since no center of tonality can survive the constant shifts of suggested keys of the preceding measures these chords are related only to each other, and it need only be noted that the augmented flavor and sequential resolution are maintained. When G flat is arrived at the sequence is completed. Obviously any of the major triads could have been established as a key center simply by continuing diatonically as the composer here chose to in G flat.

No theorist has objected to the borderline parallel octaves between melody and bass, for the slow tempo and ornate melodic line are enough to render the bass line so inconspicuously fundamental that its duplication of the essential melodic tones is not disturbing.

The illustration is not a complete picture of the score: it is not possible to accurately portray on two staves every detail of the dramatic roles of Cio-Cio San, her two part chorus of soprano friends, an American diplomat, and the accompanying orchestra. Tremolos, octave doublings, and other orchestral reinforcements are obscured or omitted in our reduction but the complete harmonic structure is shown.

A more intricate harmonic progression is seen in sequence in Example 84. It differs from the Puccini example in that it returns to the key of its opening, the interval at which the sequences occur is a minor third, and its harmonic motive consists of a chord progression rather than a chord connection.

EXAMPLE 84. Wagner, *Tannhaüser,* "Pilgrims Chorus"

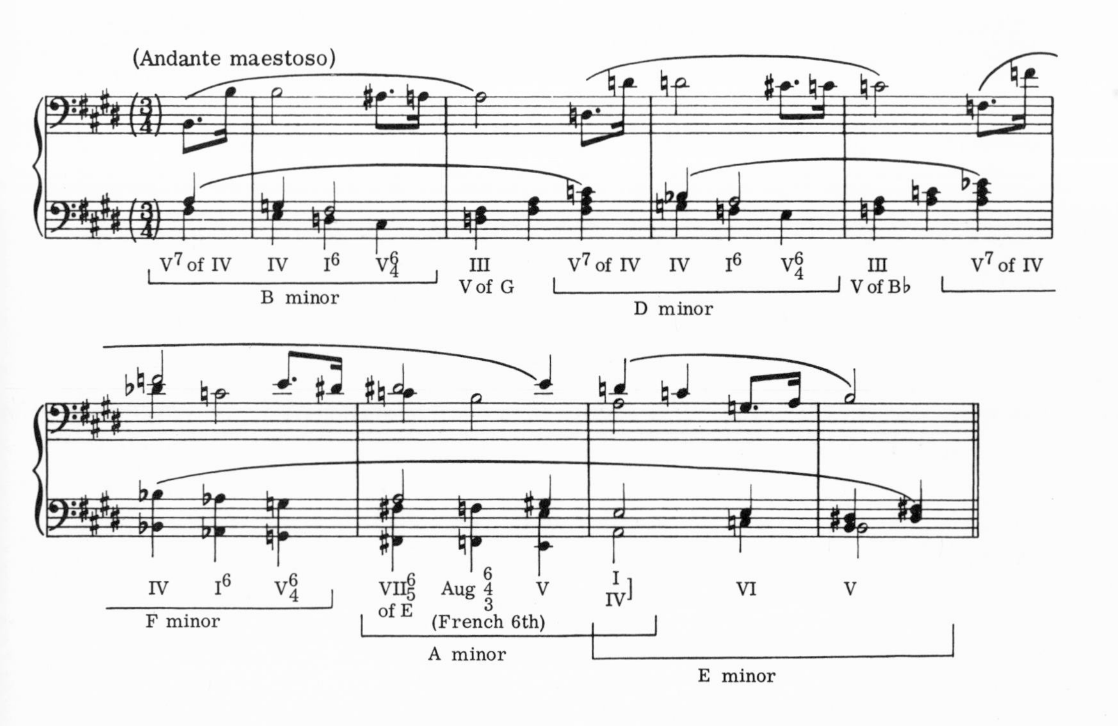

The tonal region which precedes the beginning of our quotation is B major, for the sixteen measure section which comes before begins in E and arrives at a strong dominant cadence just before our analysis begins.

A progression of five chords, diatonic in origin but here chromatically interposed and inflected to hint at another key, occurs in sequence. The tonal centers traversed bear mediant relationships to each other but this, for present purposes, is secondary to their sequential connection. Careful study of the first five chords of the example will show how simple is the way of genius. Wagner has seized upon the weak spot of the minor mode, the ambiguous and distracting chord on the third scale step. As a major triad it is tenuously suspected by the ear to be a dominant, and the composer lingers over it for three beats—longer than any other chord in the quotation. Its dominant role is proclaimed by the addition of the seventh on the third beat of its duration and we find ourselves in the mediant key, a minor third above. This device is used three times, and the third occurrence of the progression is complicated by chromaticism, as though surfeited by the diatonic, and plunges toward the cadence. The cadence brings us back to the center of polarity: E major, and we realize that we have experienced a truly tonal-chromatic event.

These two illustrations of sequential chromaticism serve only to demonstrate that an unlimited variety of harmonic devices may be utilized in sequence. Puccini's use of but one chromatic quality in the process of changing the tonal center and Wagner's use of mediant and minor-major relationships in the complex harmonic structure which leads back to the preestablished key are indications of the diversity of purposes and procedures served by harmonic sequences.

XXIV

Melodic Harmony

EVERY HARMONIC STRUCTURE—chord, resolution, progression, and sequence—described in the foregoing chapters is a result of a melodic concept. Though termed voice-leading in its participation in harmony, the quality of *melos* (a term which implies more than the popularly understood "melody: the predominant tune") is the element which is surely the heart of music; and the melodic coincidences presented as chords in this book are only those unanimously and most frequently utilized by the composers whose accomplishments have prompted this study.

This chapter is an attempt to demonstrate that the quality of melos has often brought about vertical combinations of tones which appear to be chords but do not function according to normal harmonic procedures and are heard as concurrent melodic lines or a non-harmonic melodic line superimposed over a recognizable chord: melodic harmony.

Example 85 appears to be a theoretically conceived chromatic chord progression. Each chord can be defined in a tonal region related to F major; only an occasional B flat, A, and G bass tone need be classified as a non-harmonic pedal point. It is a good subject for study and should be thoroughly analyzed for it includes Neapolitan relationships, harmonic sequence, altered chord qualities, and expanded chords.

EXAMPLE 85

It is hoped that a suspicion of something amiss is felt when the beat-by-beat labeling of these chords is completed. Too many chord connections are not chord progressions and the overly deliberate rhythm is unconvincing.

A more gratifying summary of the basic harmonic events is given below and should be similarly analyzed.

EXAMPLE 86

Comparison of these two progressions shows that the gist and gesture of the essential harmonic idea of the forty-one chords of the first is adequately represented in the eleven chords of the second. Obviously many of the tones and chords of Example 85, though readily recognizable as members of triads, seventh and ninth chords, are not essential to the progression. Thus it must be admitted that the study of harmony is not a magic key which will open the door to complete conversance with the technics of tone manipulation: counterpoint is always present and likely to dominate at any moment.

The submerged quality of melos which underlies these perusals of harmonic distillations is not a result of these progressions: it is their cause. Example 85 is the harmonic picture presented when each sixteenth of each measure of Example 3 is viewed as a chord of quarter note duration, and Example 86 is a more revealing portrayal of the harmonic relationships of Example 3, Chapter I. It is hoped that the discerning student finds this paragraph superfluous.

This rather drastic and perhaps too violent translation of contrapuntal music into purely harmonic tones clearly indicates that simultaneous melodies may so strongly dominate a texture that harmonic considerations become secondary.

The fundamental conduct of chromatic tones—sharps resolve upward, flats resolve downward, and chromatic tones resolve in the direction of their inflection or according to a diatonic relationship—is seen to be the guiding factor in the spelling of all chromatic chords. Exceptions occur only in some (not all) exceptional resolutions. The ear cannot distinguish between an augmented sixth and a minor seventh or between a minor third and an augmented second but these intervals are chosen to be notated because of their melodic tendencies. The sounds of the three possible diminished seventh chords and the four possible augmented triads, for example, are wholly enigmatic to the ear unless resolved, and to the eye unless notated according to their melodic tendencies.

The orchestra has usually completed its performance of the passage represented in Example 87 before the audience is seated, but let us pretend we have arrived early enough to give it our attention.

EXAMPLE 87. Gounod: *Faust,* Introduction

After the fortissimo request for attention is sounded a chromatic episode suggesting mystery is heard. Measure two implies only I and V chords, but measure three consists of an enharmonically spelled A flat major triad resolving to a chromatic dominant in a tritone relationship. G sharp instead of A flat is written because the composer felt it to be the leading tone to A natural. The dominant is spelled as V^7 of G because, assuming the possible imminence of the circle of fifths, it has a tenuous status as the dominant of the dominant of the dominant and because its tones are resolved melodically: F sharp and D natural as leading tones, C as a common tone, and A flat to G as the second scale step to tonic of the G implied by the upper voice.

Measures four and five provide an elementary lesson on the notation of chromatic scales, again illustrating the universal reluctance to chromatically lower the dominant. The last half of measure five does not imply eventual resolution of a half-diminished seventh chord or minor triad with minor seventh: the melodic power of the ascending chromatic scale outweighs these harmonic coincidences.

The sixth measure is simple: I of C, II^6_5 of C minor. Measure seven is similar—identical if only letter names are considered—but the chord on the fourth beat appears to be an enharmonically spelled V^7 of B flat. B flat, however, is nowhere in evidence and D sharp is not the enharmonic fourth scale step in that key but is the leading tone to E natural, the third of the chord of resolution. F, A natural, and C form the subdominant triad of the key of C, and the cadential effect is plagal.

If considered out of context this F, A, C, D sharp chord would appear to be the German Sixth of A, but as the key of A is no more a factor in the passage than B flat the composer's melodic use of these tones to precede the dominant chord at the semicadence is successful: melody overcomes the harmonic precedents. It may be wise to point out that such progressions can occur only in a strongly established tonality to which the melodic-chromatic element is utterly foreign. During the era of profuse chromaticism "utterly foreign" chords occur regularly but are found to be quite domestic when they resolve. Consequently tonal centers are strongly and unquestionably authoritative chiefly at cadential sections of musical works, and the harmonic events presently being considered are most frequently seen to occur after the effect of return to the tonic has been accomplished. Two such occurrences are shown in Example 88.

Example 88. Massenet: *Sous Les Branches.*

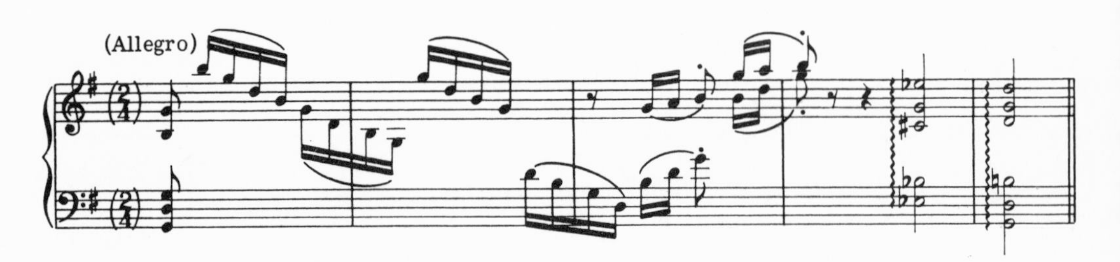

MacDowell, *Scotch Poem*

After the final cadence of his song Massenet extends the tonic chord by means of an arpeggiated pattern. The I chord is reaffirmed, preceded by the triad on the lowered sixth degree (see Chapter VI) with the superimposed leading tone to the chord fifth. MacDowell also uses the leading tone to the fifth of the tonic chord with the triad on VI, but the mode is minor and the VI diatonic and inverted. The bass tone throughout the quotation may be considered a tonic pedal point.

More complex because chromatically more extended, more daring in the persistence of remote sounding tone combinations, and more delightfully novel because it is the work of a most adventurous "Classical" composer is Example 89.

EXAMPLE 89. Haydn: Quartet, Op. 64 No. 2, Menuetto

B minor is the prevailing tonality in the measures which precede, and the quotation is an illustration of Haydn's way of dramatizing a cadence without changing the key. The Neapolitan Sixth is sounded through measures one and two and in measure three (review Chapter XVI) the leading tone of the key is sounded with it. The lower voices move up, quite logically, by step under the leading tone and in so doing sound, perhaps accidentally, the pitches of the dominant seventh chord of E♭ major. Harmonically E flat major and its dominant seventh chord have no status in B minor, but contrapuntally these pitches are as welcome as their individual tendencies toward resolution are inherent in their roles as scale tones in closely related keys. Their melodic appropriateness is disarmingly demonstrated as this unique series of chromatic harmonies converges on the I^6_4 of measure six. At first glance the doubled tonic in the I^6_4 seems strange, but listening and reflection indicate that Haydn was concerned with the disposition of tones at the point of the resolution to V, and the F sharp on the third beat of measure six is the doubled fifth which becomes the doubled root of the dominant in the following measure.

Melodic-harmony, self-contradictory term that it is, is nonetheless fitting as descriptive of a seemingly contradictory state of affairs, for the simultaneous sounds of harmony and the consecutive sounds of melody are inextricably intermingled in the musical situations discussed in this chapter. If the quotations from the literature of music which appear in the preceding chapters are reexamined it will be seen that the two are never wholly separated.

XXV

Twelve Tone Tonality

HARMONY, in reality hardly more than a method of describing the most frequent concurrences of three and four voice contrapuntal events, has at times been able to assert itself as an almost self-sufficient element in music. If all the harmonic progressions of the eighteenth and nineteenth-century literature could be tabulated it would be seen that diatonic harmony mingled with the chromatic procedures described in the first few chapters of this book occupy the vast majority of measures. Exceptional harmonic structures and resolutions require more explanation than is consistent with their frequency of occurrence. After all these generations of use in logical and familiar environments, triads and seventh chords have earned individual and often quite separate identities. As suggested above, instances of this independence are rare.

Within the frame of tonality the thought of unfettered and irresponsible chords is rather shocking, but let us look at the way of master composers in their use of this most treacherous of harmonic resources.

An operatic work of the last decade of the nineteenth century provides our first example. Although it is a dramatization of a children's story it is by no means a simple work and represents an advanced stage in the development of chromatic tonality.

EXAMPLE 90. Humperdinck: *Hansel and Gretel,* Act III

The descending chromatic scale is the subject after the positively sounded dominant of G minor. Its harmonization is arbitrary: the G major, B flat augmented, D minor, and E major triads do not suggest or recall a diatonic source. Roman numerals could be used to identify these chords only if the one useful function of Roman numerals—to describe diatonic relationships with a terminology common to all keys—is abrogated. The remoteness of the harmony of measures two and three obscure the status of the G minor tonic triad on the first beat of measure four. The dominant pedal point helps to reclaim the tonal center, and the chords which follow, though they hint at other regions, lead to the clearly cadential inverted dominant.

An earlier indication of harmonic independence is seen in Example 91. Chopin, having arrived at the tonic (F minor) triad after an intensely dramatic scene, dissolves the key in an almost frantic series of hammered chords.

EXAMPLE 91. Chopin: *Ballade,* Op. 52

It is possible to find a diatonic source for each of these chord connections, but the value of such painstaking categorization is questionable, for the musical intent and effect is kaleidoscopic.

The key is reentered at the end of measure three of the quotation and the composer, as though attempting to compensate for the preceding upheaval, proclaims the dominant key (V, V^7 of V, V in measure five), pauses, and then dwells on the dominant pedal point over which the V, V^7 of V, V^7, II^7, and V chords are gently sounded. This passage shows the adventurous spirit of Romanticism and the Classicist's caution. The first three measures point toward developments which led to results such as Example 92 and from measure four to the end of the excerpt the almost diatonic deliberations remind us of the Classical preoccupation with clarity of tonality. Such striking contrasts are not commonplace, even in the dramatic tumult of Romanticism.

By the end of the nineteenth century, semi-random chord progressions had become routine to *avante-garde* fanciers and were well on the way to a place in the store of standard harmonic devices. Example 92 is a fragment of a daring and up-to-date work of 1910.

EXAMPLE 92. R. Strauss: *Der Rosenkavalier,* Act I

The three note figure which opens the quotation, and recurs after the third beats of measure two, four, and nine, includes the only suggestion of non-harmonic matters: every other tone is a member of a familiar triad or seventh chord. The tonality is clearly established and never contradicted, but the chord-to-chord progression seems to deny the key, the grammar of harmony, and the gospel of melos.

If we listen, think, and remember as musicians must we will hear the first two measures lead from I to V; realize that the tones and chords which bridge the octave and a half are simply filling in space; and remember that non-harmonic tones and arpeggiated chords have performed a similar service before.

Measures three and four extend the progression past the V^4_2 and pause on the half diminished seventh chord on C sharp; II^7 of B minor, VII^7 of D major, a traditional chromatic participant in G major, and a chord of instability, rich coloration, and ambiguity. Mediant relationships follow, and after the G, E flat, and F sharp triads a most awkward appearing sequence is heard. The arpeggiated F sharp major chord brings on a parallel harmonic sequence which includes only half-diminished and dominant $^6_5$ quality chords. The root progression is symmetrical—the down a minor third, down a minor second pattern is repeated four times—and descends the octave. The uppermost line, hardly melodic, contributes much to the sense of unorthodoxy with its major seventh leaps. The precipitate flavor of this series of eight chords is eliminated by the lengthened note values of the final pair but the angular contour of the upper voice is preserved in the resolution to the dominant seventh and its resolution to the tonic. This traditional cadence is further ornamented by the recurrence of the opening three note motive in the octave below that of its first appearance.

Complicated as it appears to be, this Example is only a much elaborated I-V-I progression, for there are no other tonal suggestions present. In broad outline it is a three part harmonic structure: I to V in the first two measures, I past V to a point of suggested departure in measures three and four, and a refusal of departure and a general instability (unresolved $^6_4$ chords and the mediant sequence) subsiding inevitably into the tonal cadence. The I to V of part one is expanded by the interjection of diminished and half-diminished chords between the tonal harmonies. The painter who does not use green paint from the tube to paint grass but applies tiny strokes of blue and yellow and perhaps a touch of red and brown to show the multiplicity of color in grass, is using the same device. The painter does not intend or expect our close inspection of his means of intensifying the experience of viewing grass; and the composer will be equally surprised at any marvelling at his method of progressing from tonic to dominant.

The first quotation of music in this book consisted of tonic and dominant chords in association with chromatic non-harmonic tones. In Example 92 chromatic tones are woven into the structure and appear to be harmonic; the tonality which sounds is E major and the chords which establish the key are, as in Example I, tonic and dominant.

The coincidence of composers' names is not the only point of similarity between these two most dissimilar compositions. The inescapable authority of tonality prevails in both as well as in each of the illustrative examples of music which separate them. The twelve tones of the chromatic scale, present in the three examples of Chapter I, are present in the three Examples of this Chapter also. We have traced their progress from a purely ornamental role as melodic embellishments to their status as full participants in the common practice of tonal harmony.

XXVI

Conclusion

STUDENTS EXPECT RULES, but in music there are no rules and no systems. There is only the dazzling and awesome heritage and reality of musical sound. All who would add to or draw conclusions from analysis of the literature do so by emphasizing, minimizing, magnifying, ignoring, or isolating some aspects of the art.

Aware of the danger, we offer a set of rules and a challenge. The cumulative effect of the discussions of chromaticism presented in this text surely indicate that any chord may resolve to any chord. The rules which seem to govern even the most bizarre chord connections are summarized here.

1. There is usually at least one common tone between the two chords. If so, it is retained in the same voice or repeated in the octave above or below.
2. All voices except the one or two common-tone-bearers move by step. Less frequently short leaps occur.
3. The voices do not all move in the same direction. Here again octave transpositions may confuse the eye but not the ear.

4. The chromatic or diatonic inflection of a tone of the first chord is not contradicted by a tone of the second chord. This is the rule which warns against cross relations, sometimes violated as described in Chapter VIII.
5. Parallel perfect fifths, octaves, and unisons do not occur between any two voices. (If a resolution of a chord which may be interpreted as a German Sixth is involved this rule may also be modified.)

Parallelism, abrupt sequences, and purely pictorial sound effects excepted, these rules are a prescription for the connection of utterly random selections of harmonic structures. Try them! this is the challenge. Try to find a new combination of chords.

This is the turning point, perhaps the grim realization of satiety. In capsule form it is part of the dilemma which confronts contemporary creative musicians when the achievements of nineteenth-century composers are examined.

Reflections of this summation of tonal harmony can be seen in subsequent developments of musical technic. The study of twentieth-century devices, essential for twentieth-century musicians, cannot be undertaken unless the nineteenth-century roots of modern practice are mastered. Such study will show that twentieth-century melody, harmony, rhythm, form, and tone colors are hard put to equal the perfection of proportion among these acknowledged elements of music so evident in the works of nineteenth-century masters.

It is noteworthy that texts on harmony are more numerous than texts on any other element of music. The reason is clear: only harmony includes all the other elements. Melody guides the voice-leading, rhythm paces its movement, sequences are diminutive representatives of form, and color is the medium by which the sounds come to our ears. More modern facets, even the apparent diffusions of musical expressiveness implied by radical experimentation, may be approached only from a standpoint of familiarity with the language of the musical era from which they grew.

But after all technicalities, precedents, and recommended procedures have been digested—music remains a personal language. Each of the technics of the art can be mastered by all who possess talent, intelligence, and perseverance; but it is a small minority of strongly individual personalities which has set the standards and created the works which we consider definitive musical monuments.

Discover your own uses for this knowledge—it is valuable only as it becomes a resource which your own musicianship uses to express itself. If you possess the gift of music you have an obligation to demonstrate your service to art through honest and enlightened performance.

Appendix

APPENDIX

Popular Music

IT MAY SEEM ODD that so much of the musical content of twentieth-century theatre, dance, motion pictures, radio, television, balladry, and general practice speaks, with only minor modifications, in the tonal harmonic language described in this book. The modifications will be discussed but it must first be understood that this Appendix is included only because the twentieth-century music of which we speak is a living demonstration of the validity of the procedures described in the text proper. The fashions and fads of popular music are not our concern. We seek only to describe the adaptation of this vocabulary to the everyday service of such a wide diversity of arts and enterprises. Recognition of it is justified by its universal and unquestioned acceptance by the public and, less obviously, by its often slightly selfconscious acceptance by the musically literate in moments of relaxation.

Some basic aspects of the practice of popular music follow.

TERMINOLOGY

The chord symbols used are developed from guitar (and ukelele) notation. The guitar is a complicated instrument, and rather than attempt to arrange each chord to fit the instrument's six strings and the player's four useable fingers the chords may simply be named. Example A shows the method.

EXAMPLE A

The diagonal dashes represent the beats of the measures and the guitarist is trusted to play the appropriate chord on the appropriate beat. Such symbols (without the dashes) often appear above the top line of piano arrangements of popular songs, and although intended for a fretted string instrument are often mistakenly assumed to be harmonic reductions of the composition. The fallacy of this assumption is twofold: first, because of the complexity of the instrument many complicated chords cannot be sounded in an acceptable position and the guitarist is given only part of the chord to play. Example B is typical.

EXAMPLE B

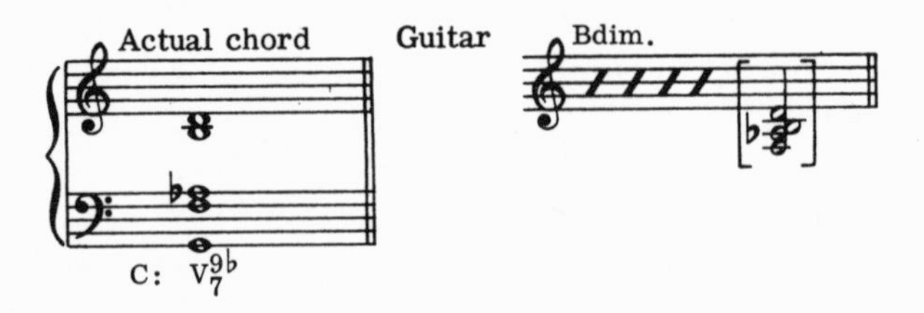

The second drawback is that the bass tone is not indicated nor is any counterpoint or voice-leading implied.

Nevertheless the ease with which vertical chord structures can be identified has made this terminology the—lamentably—only harmonic vocabulary of too many instrumentalists.

The following describes the symbols as they are understood by musicians who use them, and each is illustrated in Example C.

Example C

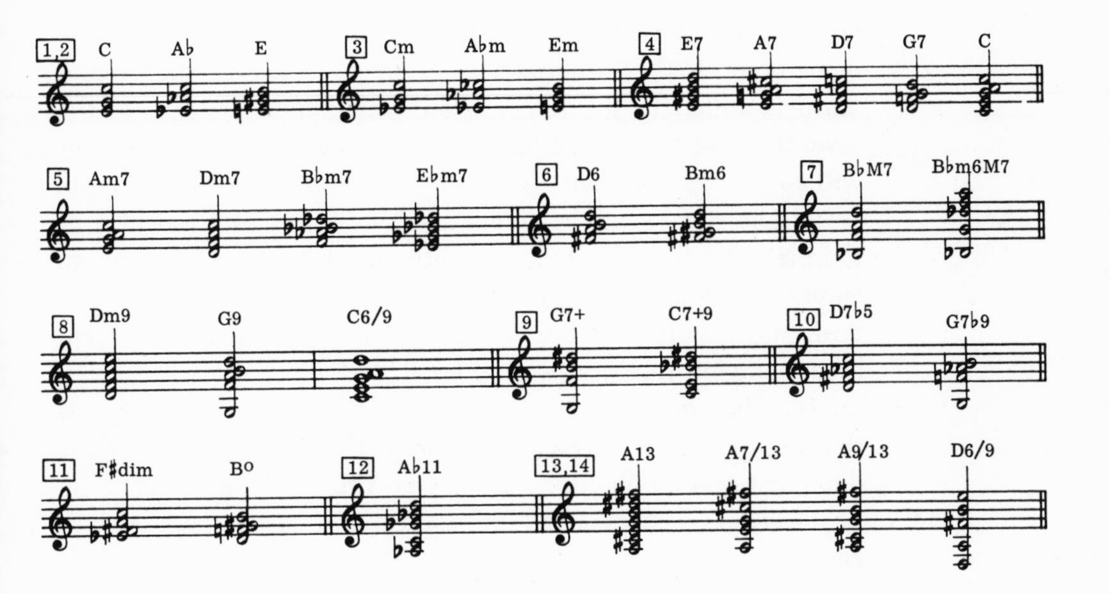

The chords are shown in close position for convenience. The symbols do not imply any spacing of tones or their resolution.

1. The given letter (note name: E flat, F sharp, A, etc.) is the root.

2. A letter alone indicates a major triad on that root.

3. A small letter "m" following the note name indicates that the triad is minor in quality.

4. The numeral 7 following the letter indicates that a minor seventh is added to the major triad, forming a chord of dominant seventh quality.

5. The numeral 7 following a small "m" indicates that a minor seventh is added to the minor triad, forming a chord of the quality of II^7, III^7 and VI^7 of the major mode.

6. The numeral 6 following a letter or a small "m" indicates that a major sixth is added to the triad. If the triad is major it is simply an added sixth, but if the triad is minor a chord of the quality of II^7 in minor and VII^7 in major is formed.

7. A capital "M" indicates that the interval named *after* the capital "M" is major.

8. The numeral 9 following a letter indicates that a major ninth is added to the dominant seventh quality chord on the named root. If the 9 follows a small "m" it indicates that a major ninth is added to the minor triad with minor seventh. If the seventh is not to be included the 9 will not follow the letter but will follow the number, usually 6, which replaces the seventh.

9. The sign + or the term "aug." indicates that the fifth of the major triad or dominant seventh chord is raised, forming an augmented triad or an augmented dominant quality chord. The term "aug." with a number other than 7 indicates that the interval accompanying the term is raised a half step.

10. The sign "♭" or — (minus sign) before a number indicates that the interval is lowered a half step. This sign is used to show dominant quality chords with lowered fifths and/or ninths.

11. Dim, d. or a small "o" indicates a diminished seventh chord.

12. The numeral 11 indicates that the minor seventh, major ninth and augmented eleventh are added to the major triad. (The chord fifth may be omitted.)

13. The numeral 13 indicates the presence of the 13th above the seventh of a diatonic or chromatic dominant seventh chord. The major ninth and augmented eleventh may also be included: the effect must be tested in context.

14. When two or more numerals appear after the note name no tones other than those indicated by these numerals are included.

There are very few harmonic situations likely to occur in the popular harmonic idiom which cannot be specifically described by this terminology. If purely contrapuntal events transpire, or any other non-harmonic texture is employed this system of harmonic identification is obviously rendered superfluous and is abandoned.

A now rarely used symbol, a rather surprising evidence of the persistence of contrapuntal assertiveness, is the term "sus. 4." This sign indicates a suspension, the interval of a perfect fourth replacing the third of a major triad or dominant seventh quality chord; and the chord which follows invariably permits resolution of this dissonance. Its obsolescence (its replacement is shown in Example F 8[e]) is due to the recognition of the fact that this is a system of harmonic description only and *only* harmonic structures are admissible.

This terminology serves its purpose well. Its limitations are many: it does not aid in the construction of a true bass line, it offers no clue to the role of individual chords or chord tones, and by its noncommital efficiency minimizes the importance of the other musical elements, none of which has had the benefit of such an all inclusive shorthand.

It should be noted however that this seemingly superficial system of harmonic nomenclature, developed by practical musicians for practical purposes, makes no distinction between diatonic and chromatic harmony. It is capable of describing highly chromatic chord connections without furor and renders even a key signature superfluous.

THE CHORDS

Perhaps the most startling harmonic aspect of this idiom is the fact that there are no triads. Never are fewer than four individual pitches admissible, and the level of relative consonance is raised to the point at which the interval of a second is accepted by all ears as an element of truly tonic harmony. As pointed out in Chapter XXII, it is possible to increase the pitch membership of chords without altering their function, and the style now under discussion very definitely adheres to that principle.

There are only four functional chord structures: major quality, minor quality, dominant quality, and diminished quality. Augmented chords exist only as modifications of the dominant quality, and minor seventh and sixth chords are simply dissonant forms of minor quality chords.

There is no provision for unusual spelling. All chords are made of superimposed thirds, and such structures as augmented sixth chords are disguised. The German Sixth appears as a simple dominant seventh chord; the French Sixth as a dominant seventh with flatted fifth. The Italian Sixth and Neapolitan Sixth, chords of three tones, are not used. The general rules and principles of voice-leading and the resolution of dissonance remain in effect, however, for this is a style which grew from sound. The higher level of consonance permits a liberal view of the resolution of dissonance. Chord sevenths, for example, may resolve by step in either direction if the texture is consistently rich in intervals of a second. Notation is a wholly secondary consideration.

The chord structures described below are classified according to their function, and even if the texture is thickened to include chords of as many as six pitches their tonal function will remain. Only consistency of texture is essential: a six tone chord is rarely effective if preceded and followed by four voice chords. Typical progressions usually consist of four and five tone chords.

Inversions are rare because of the profusion of pitches in each chord. The identity of the chord may be obscured by the sound of a strong interval such as a perfect fifth or fourth between the bass (not the root) and an upper tone.

I. Major triads
   (a) The root, third, and fifth remain present and unaltered.
   (b) The major sixth is usually added as fourth tone.

(c) The major seventh is occasionally added as fourth tone. It sounds non-harmonic if placed a minor second below the root and is thus usually found a true seventh (or an octave and a seventh) above the root.

(d) The major ninth may be added as fifth tone. It must not appear as a second above the root and is usually above the third.

(e) The root, fifth, or, less commonly, the third may be doubled if a preestablished texture is to be maintained.

II. Minor Triads

(a) The root, third, and fifth remain present and unaltered.

(b) If the chord resolves up a major second to a dominant quality chord (as in IV to V in minor) or if it is the center of the prevailing tonality the major sixth is added as fourth tone.

(c) If the chord resolves down a perfect fifth or up a perfect fourth, or if it is a II^7, III^7 or VI^7 in major, the minor seventh is added as fourth tone.

(d) The major ninth may be added as fifth tone. It must not appear a second from the root and is usually above the third.

(e) The root, third or fifth may be doubled as sixth tone.

(f) If the chord is a II^7 which resolves to V^7 the perfect eleventh is occasionally added as the uppermost tone.

III. Dominant Quality Chords

(a) The root, major third, and minor seventh remain present and unaltered.

(b) The perfect, augmented, or diminished fifth may be added as fourth, fifth, or sixth tone. If the augmented fifth is used it must appear above the seventh.

(c) The major, minor, or augmented ninth may be added as fourth, fifth, or sixth tone. The major and minor ninth may appear above or below the third, the augmented ninth only above it.

(d) The thirteenth may be added as fourth, fifth, sixth, or seventh tone. It must appear above the seventh and at least a ninth above the fifth if present. The thirteenth is not used if the chord includes an augmented fifth.

(e) The augmented eleventh may be added as fifth, sixth or seventh tone. It is not used if the chord contains a diminished or augmented fifth.

IV. Diminished chords

(a) All four tones may be present as the first four tones.

(b) Any one of the first four tones, usually the uppermost tone, may be replaced by its own upper neighbor (a major second above).

(c) Tones may be added a major ninth above one or two of the original four chord tones as fifth or sixth tones.

(d) No two tones may be a second apart in (b) or (c) above.

Example D illustrates these points and Example E shows a simple harmonic phrase expanded to include five and six voices. The five and six voice versions of Example E are arranged in an arpeggiated pattern because for our present purpose it is well to hear as well as see the structures tone by tone. It may be mentioned that the D sharp (augmented ninth) of the dominant of the six voice example may have been written as E flat by a practitioner of the style (as a passing tone between the preceding E and the following D). Conversely, the A flat in the dominant of the five voice version is an enharmonic augmented fifth spelled according to common practice, perhaps common because of the frequent use of simultaneous major and minor thirds above the root in the closely related "blues" style.

EXAMPLE D

1 Four, five and six tone major chords:
2 Four, five and six tone minor chords resolved:
3 Four tone dominant chords resolved:
Five tones:
Six tones:
4 Diminished chords resolved:

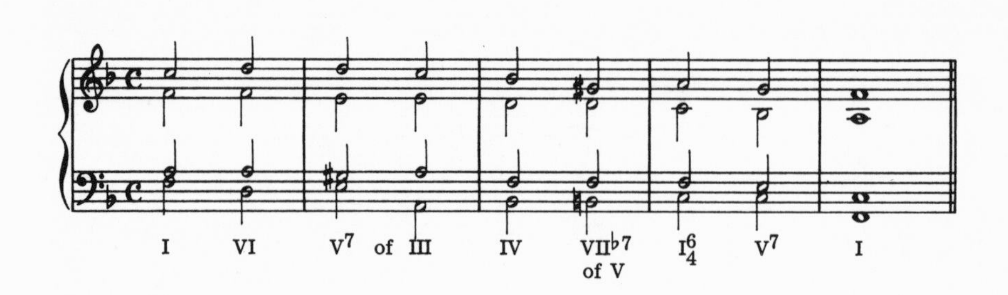
I
VI
V7 of III
IV
VII♭7 of V
I 6 4
V7
I

Example E

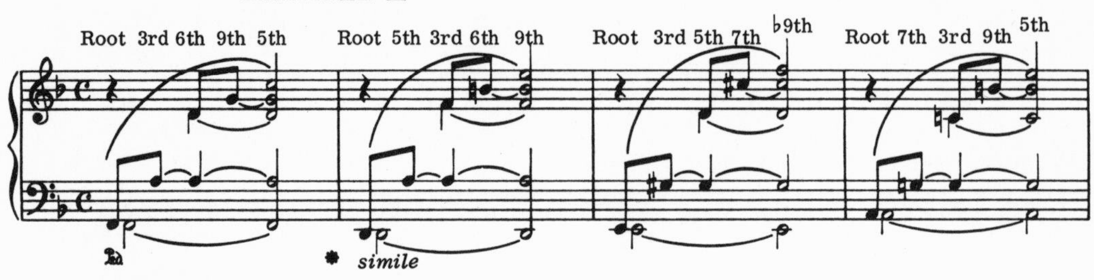
Root 3rd 6th 9th 5th
Root 5th 3rd 6th 9th
Root 3rd 5th 7th ♭9th
Root 7th 3rd 9th 5th
simile

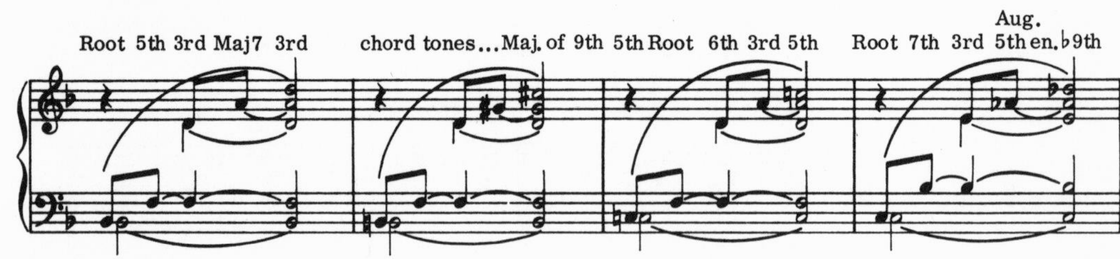
Root 5th 3rd Maj7 3rd
chord tones...Maj. of 9th 5th
Root 6th 3rd 5th
Root 7th 3rd Aug. 5th en. ♭9th

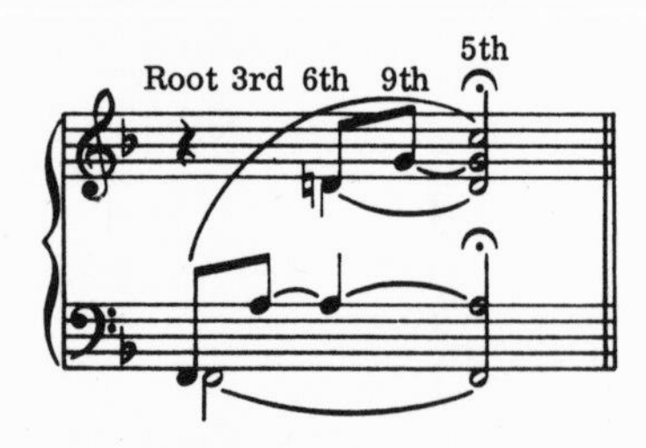
Root 3rd 6th 9th 5th

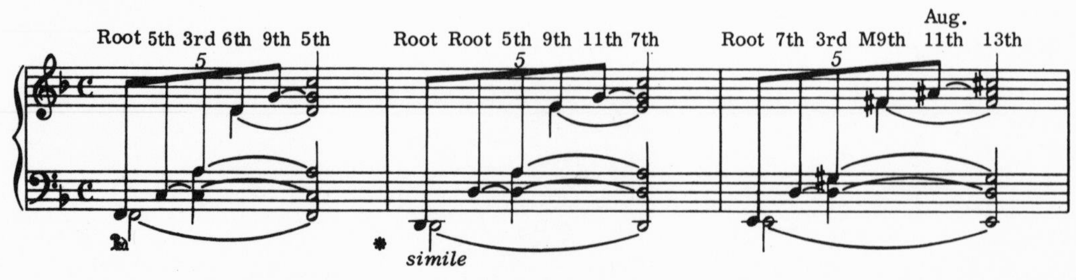
Root 5th 3rd 6th 9th 5th
5
Root Root 5th 9th 11th 7th
5
Root 7th 3rd M9th Aug. 11th 13th
5
simile

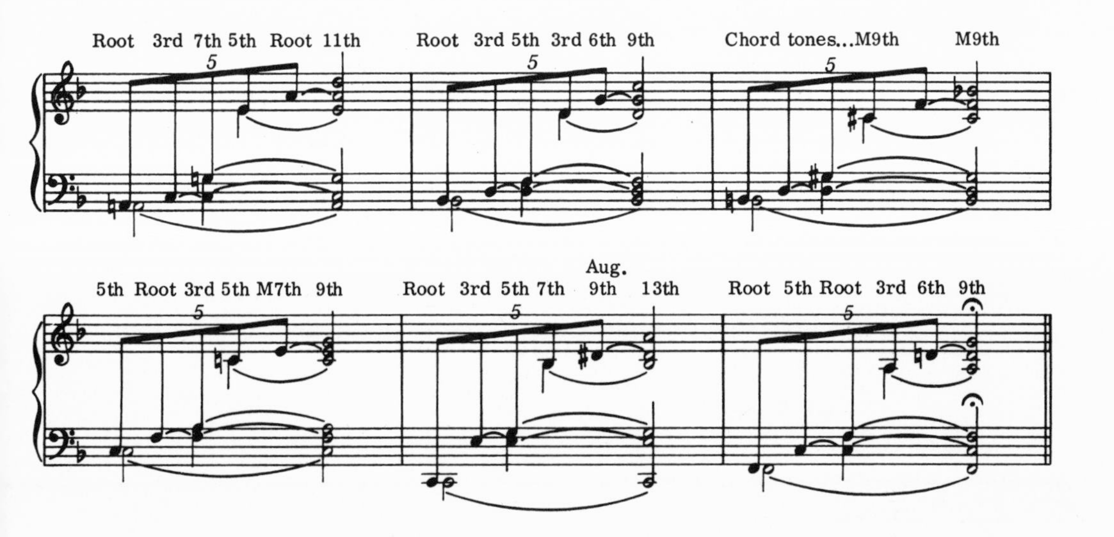

HARMONIC MELODY

In spite of the rather lurid and mechanical harmonic routine described above the essence of the style is two part: melody and bass. The bass line is identical to all harmonic bass lines, consisting mainly of chord roots and occasional inversions to approximate melodic contours, but the melody is delivered with its harmonic support attached. The nonmelodic chord tones are completely dependent upon the melodic line for their duration and direction of movement. The tendencies to resolve of leading tones, chord sevenths, suspensions, etc., are ignored as are the general rules of voice-leading.

This rather drastic departure from traditional practice is governed by a strict set of rules, necessitated by the fact that if their identification with the melody is lost the harmonic voices will assume a melodic identity of their own in violation of the style and texture.

The basic concept requires that each melody tone be the uppermost tone of a chord of four pitches (four different letter-names) contained within the octave, i.e., the widest possible interval between the melody tone and the lowest chord tone is a major seventh.

The rules which guide in the accomplishment of this feat without the sacrifice of tonality, harmonic rhythm, or clarity of chord quality and function are given below and illustrated in Example F. The numbering in the example and in the summary corresponds.

Example F

6
Am7 D7 G Am7 D7 G
7 a
G7 C G7 C C C C7
G7
b
F
c
B♭ UN LN UN LN LN F7 LN LN
(dim7) (Par.) (dim7) (dim7) (dom.7) (Par.) (dim.7)
LN B♭
d
E♭ F♯dim
(dim7)
e
D7 Gsus4 G D7 G D7 (Am7) G D7 (Cm6) G

1. Major triads contain the added major sixth. The major seventh is used instead of the sixth when it is the melody tone and when its use permits stepwise motion instead of repetition.
2. Minor triads contain the minor seventh or major sixth as described in II(b) and (c) above.
3. Diatonic and chromatic dominant seventh chords contain the third and seventh. The upper tone (melody) may be any tone of the chromatic scale except the tone a perfect fourth above the root or the tone a half step below its root. These two tones are treated as non-harmonic in dominant harmony. The root may be omitted and replaced by the major or minor ninth.
4. Diminished seventh chords contain all four tones.
5. Dominant seventh chords with augmented fifth must be spaced so no three tones are contained within the interval of a diminished fourth or major third. This frequently requires that another chord be used in its place, but the substituted chord must not disturb the augmented quality of the harmony. Effective substitutions are (chords are spelled from top down):
   (a) Ninth in melody. Ninth, seventh, augmented fifth, third.
   (b) Root in melody. Root, augmented fifth, third, major ninth.
   (c) Augmented fifth in melody. No substitution necessary: augmented fifth, third, root or ninth, seventh.
   (d) Third in melody. Third, ninth, seventh, augmented fifth, or: third, root, seventh, flatted fifth.
   (e) Seventh in melody (very rare). Seventh, flatted fifth, third root.
6. Thirteenths are associated only with dominant harmony and as such are included in 3 above. The augmented eleventh in dominant chords is also shown in 3; but the perfect eleventh as it occurs with minor triads with minor seventh remains. When seen it is usually superimposed over a 11^7 chord which

resolves to V^7. If the bass tone is the dominant tone (which is not rare in cadential passages) the chord must be eleventh, root, seventh, fifth. If the bass tone is the root of the II chord, it may be eleventh, ninth, seventh, fifth.

7. Non-chord tones in melody are often higher numbered members of the prevailing chord. The upper neighbor to a chord root is the chord ninth, that of the chord sixth is the major seventh. In such cases the three lower tones may continue the chord as described above or they may move to form a diminished seventh chord or other neighboring tone structure. The effect must be tested at each occurrence.
   (a) Example 7 (a) shows a few such alternatives.
   (b) Passing tones are effectively harmonized with diminished seventh chords.
   (c) Upper neighbor notes may be harmonized with diminished seventh chords, lower neighbor notes with the parallel chord, a diminished seventh chord or a dominant or other quality chord in which all moving tones are neighbor notes.
   (d) Non-chord tones which are one step above a chord tone of a diminished seventh chord are usually harmonized with the diminished seventh chord with the next tone below the melody omitted.
   (e) Suspensions may be treated as purely melodic events, but the style and texture are then contradicted. More commonly the chord is suspended with the melody or a new chord is inserted at the point of suspension.

Other possibilities exist, and as always no aspect of music can be reduced to a set of absolute and inviolate rules. Here as elsewhere individual talents will find individual ways to cope with musical instincts confined to a fixed and definable style.

ARRANGING

The public which controls the fate of popular music gives precedence to the performer. The composer is sometimes respected but usually known only as one who provides vehicles for performance. Rarely is the work of the arranger evaluated, yet none of this music reaches the ears of its admirers until someone has arranged it—tailored it to the key, style, purpose, talent, and instrumentation of the performer or performers.

That which follows is not a detailed description of the arranger's role. It is a glance at the harmonically inspired processes described above as they are applied in actual practice.

The arranger begins with something similar to Example G1, which shows the first four measures of a "tune." Only the melody and the chord names are important to him, and from them he proceeds according to the specific requirements of his commission.

EXAMPLE G1

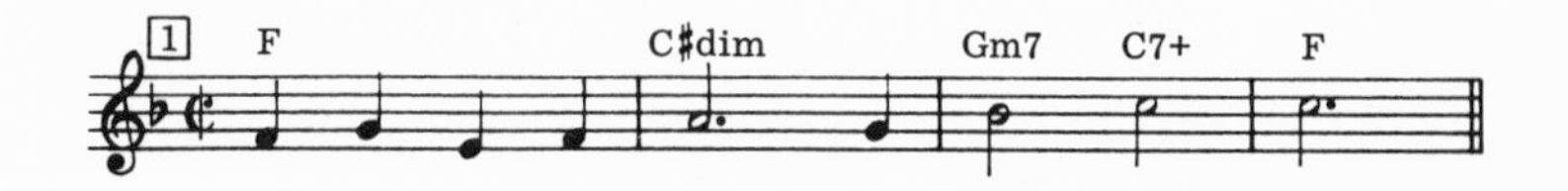

If a piano arrangement for general distribution is called for, Example G2, in which something happens on each quarter of each measure and the right hand need not be lifted from the keyboard, may be provided.

EXAMPLE G2

A more intricate version may be prepared for the more proficient amateur pianist. The chords are expanded to include more dissonance as in Example G3.

Example G3

Four voices or instruments with an independent bass may be employed. Example G4 shows how a bass and four voices, stringed instruments, saxophones, brasses, or any combination of similar toned performers can be employed.

Example G4

Example G5 shows an arrangement which utilizes the principles of harmonic melody in an accompaniment, derived from Example G3, to the sung or played melody.

Example G5

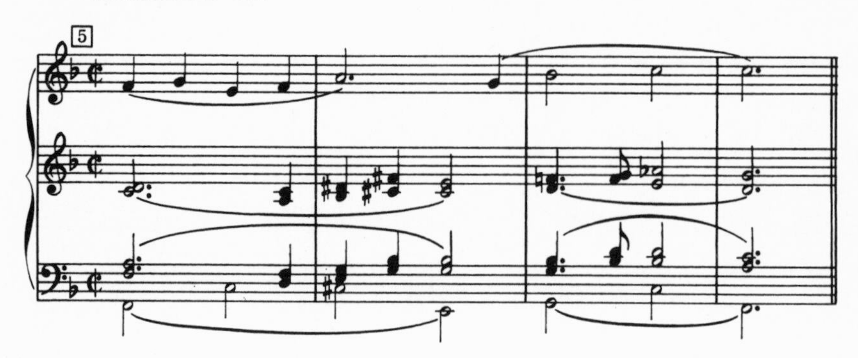

Example G6 demonstrates the reason for instrumental sections of five players. The four part harmonized melody is reinforced by lower octave doubling.

Example G6

This five part conception can be adapted to the piano. The right hand plays the four upper parts and the left hand, unable to reach the bass notes, devotes itself to the ornamented melody. Because no legato is possible in the right hand the left hand melody predominates, giving the low register the dominant voice. Example G7 shows why so many stylized pianists are heard only in association with double basses and other non-melodic instruments.

Example G7

The rules and procedures of harmonic melody, as seen in Examples G4, 5, and 6 are modified in Example G8. The chord tone next below the melody is sounded an octave below its normal position.

Example G8

This is an effective way to vary the texture when four, not five, melodic voices are available. A fifth voice doubling the melody in the lower octave here would erase the openness of the sound and unduly emphasize the tones in the lower register.

Example G8 also employs syncopation. The absolute regularity of the rhythmic pulse, here seen in bass but in performance sounded by the rhythm section (drums, piano, double bass, and guitar), permits this irregularity of motion in the upper voices. The device is simple: some tones are sounded one eighth of the measure before their normal position. Two quarter notes are rarely sounded in consecutive order as quarter notes; one or another is usually syncopated or a dotted quarter—eighth figure is substituted as in the first measure of the example. Quarter note triplets may replace any combination of three tones (quarter and eighth notes) between the first to third beats or third to following first beat.

Often heard but rarely seen is the metrical subdivision of Example G9. In the popular idiom the quarter note may be subdivided in three or two. Three is more common and the $\frac{12}{8}$ notation is usually correct but is seldom used because of the complexity of its long and intricate measures. More or less random changes from $\frac{12}{8}$ to C ($\frac{16}{8}$) are frequent.

Example G9

Improvisation is a distinctive element of popular music, and Example G9 is an attempt to show how an instrumentalist or singer may ornament and elaborate the melodic line.

Example G10 is similar but makes no attempt to approximate the melody. It is wholly concerned with the harmonic structure, and typically features higher numbered chord tones and nonharmonic tones.

Example G10

Example G9 includes an almost fundamental bass line and a guitar to sound the chords, but Example G10 consists of only an ornamented and melodic bass and a florid melody. It is obviously only the chord progression which holds the passage together, and even here where the harmonies are almost completely obscured the tonality is preserved. The idiomatic melodic style is the striking feature but it is wholly dependent upon the harmonic element.

Although the arranger has many other strings to his bow, Example G, particularly numbers 3, 4, 5, 6, and 8, accounts for a very large proportion of his output. There are other applications: Example G5 may be rearranged so the melody is treated as in Example G4 and the upper tone of the accompaniment is used as an accompanying melody an octave above. The device shown in Example G8 may be expanded and the melody may be the upper, inner, or lower tone of the four part structure. Instrumental effects can be varied by such realignments, but the logical variety of tonal harmony united with a relentlessly unvaried rhythmic pulse remains as the one all pervading condition through all the convolutions of the style.

THE FORM

Popular music in the United States is dance music and many true masterworks of music are cast in the rhythm and tempo of the dance. Many of our contemporaries are convinced that the essence of the idiom will eventually become part of the general vocabulary and formal resources of music. There have been developments beyond the devices described here but a very simple fact continues to be obvious: as creative musicians move from the dance hall to the concert hall they leave no void, for the dancing public is always provided with the pattern it seems to require. The dance musician in the concert hall finds himself competing with very great and unfettered composers and performers. If he brings only the remnants or mannered routines of an outgrown functional practice he will not fare well. If he is an artist his invention will transcend such restrictions but will then be indistinguishable from the composers and performers who have had no such restrictions to overcome and who are many, well tested, and proven—often touched with genius.

The "popular song" has a very strong influence on those whose musical careers are devoted to performing it or representations of it. It reached its zenith during the years between World Wars I and II and now seems to deserve to be called "classic," for its influence conforms to one definition of that label—the one which defines Classicism as a period in which creative artists work happily in preestablished forms as opposed to Romanticism wherein new forms of expression are sought. The great majority of the vast number of songs of the period, written by many different composers for various purposes, are identical in form: thirty-two measures (really sixteen but written at half tempo with the apologetic time signature ¢ divided into four equal phrases with regular and predictable cadences. The pattern is AABA or ABAC, and there is always a strong semicadence at the end of phrase B. The second of these designs is occasionally modified thematically but never harmonically: the cadences always arrive on schedule.

This simple form is so obvious that even the musically illiterate—those who can neither read nor write music—can unerringly compose phrases which fill it. More than one of the successful tunes of this particular golden age were so produced. The melodies must not only conform to the phrase length and form but must be limited to a range of about a tenth, superimposed over an absolutely unvaried and predetermined rhythmic pulse, restricted to note values which permit the easy pronunciation of the song-poem by the untrained, and usually made of sequential motives or diatonic scale steps even though the accompanying harmony may be quite chromatic.

This lengthy footnote to chromatic harmony consists of easily definable rules and procedures. It attempts to describe a much admired and still valid manifestation of tonal harmony even as it is confined and routinized. There are other manifestations of tonality and there are other avenues of musical expression which exist only as manifestations of the human effort and obligation to grow beyond what is known to be inexorably true. To pursue either or both of these ideas requires familiarity with all, and more than the vocabulary and grammar of the music which is the subject of this book.

Index of Musical Examples

(BY COMPOSER)

Index